Preparing for and experiencing the

CHALLENGES OF LEADERSHIP

by
Ernest Ferrell

Designed by
Ernest Ferrell

Layout by
Graphic Edge, Inc.

Tallahassee, Florida

FATHER & SON
PUBLISHING, INC.
4909 N. Monroe Street • Tallahassee, Florida 32303
www.fatherson.com • email: lance@fatherson.com
800-741-2712

"When I Am
Successful My Enemies
Grow Stronger
And My Friends
Grow Weary
And My Resolve
Grows More
Determined"

Rev. Ernest Ferrell

Two Disciplines Working
together
The Church and
the Urban League

The Church
My Christian Values
are Kingdom Building,
Accountability,
Respectability
and Leadership.

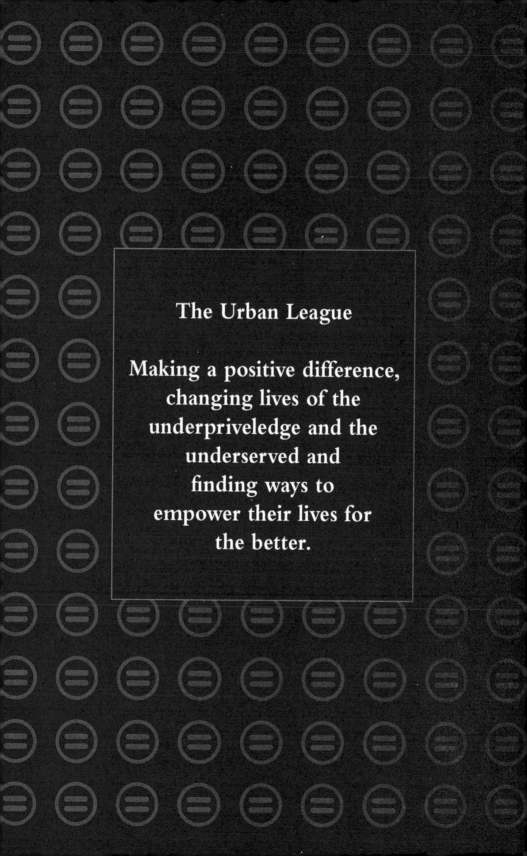

The Urban League

Making a positive difference,
changing lives of the
underpriveledge and the
underserved and
finding ways to
empower their lives for
the better.

PRAYER OF THANKSGIVING

Dear Lord Jesus, I want to thank you for my life, and a reasonable portion of health and strength. Thank you for providing me with a clear mind that I know who I am and to whom I belong. Thank you Lord Jesus for the joys and peace that you provide me daily. When I am weak you give me strength, when I am confused you give me reassurance, when I am in despair you give me hope, and when I am lonely you give me comfort. I thank you.

I thank you Lord Jesus for granting me the determination to write this book. You prepared me to write when you sent me through the many challenges which prepared me for leadership, and only your divine will fulfilled my reality. It was only your grace and your mercy which guided me through. I thank you. I pray Lord Jesus for everyone who reads my story that they will be blessed and inspired to tell their stories of how you have brought them through their challenges.

Lord teach us to cherish our shortcomings as stepping stones of maturity for the greater calling on our lives. Help us to stay focused on the brighter side of life so that whatever you take us through it is only for our good and for your glory. Finally, Lord Jesus, I pray for your peace that surpasses all understanding will be a blessing to others, and the sacrifices you made for each and everyone when you gave your only begotten son, Jesus Christ, who promised those who believe would have eternal life. Thank you. Amen

*"You have not chosen
me but I have chosen you
and ordained you that you
should go forth and
bring forth fruit and that
your fruit should remain
that whatsoever you shall ask
the Father in my name
he shall give
it to you"*

John 15:16
King James Version of the Bible

Foreword

By

Bishop Adam J. Richardson

If there is anyone who is credentialed by the school of pragmatic leadership to write a book with the title Preparing for and Experiencing the Challenges of Leadership, it would have to be Ernest Ferrell. His roles as a visionary pastor, community leader, former denominational head, and forward-thinking president/CEO of the Tallahassee Urban League qualify him to share his insights with the world. In fact, the insights from this memoir are long overdue.

Writing an autobiography is often as dangerous as it is a challenge. Making a judgment about what to leave out is as critical as what to leave in. What Ernest Ferrell has decided to share are the essentials of his life's journey. There is enough here to maintain our interest, and also a good deal to teach us. These are the bare bones on which the leadership muscle, brilliance, and personality have been attached. Here are the essential ports-of-call on his journey and the lessons learned along the way. I value the friendship and professional camaraderie we have maintained and enjoyed over the span of years now approaching fifty. Though I have been negligent in telling him so, I have always admired his capacity to do so many things well. It's nigh time that he would tell the rest of us how he does it.

Actually, I'm reasonably certain that I know how he does it. It's his faith! He is steeped in an undaunted belief that God is real. His life is guided by principles articulated in the teachings of Jesus, sustained in the acceptance of what Christ accomplished at Calvary, and his daily experience with the power and Spirit of God. In this regard, I have

9

also valued his ecumenical attitude and spirit. He is an Elder and a seasoned pastor in the Primitive Baptist Church, but he is also at home across denominational lines with a healthy respect for the variety of other faith traditions. I suspect, therefore, that it is his faith that has sustained him through the "trials and tribulations" of leadership. This memoir reveals not only his successes at leadership, but also his wounds and disappointments. He has demonstrated a capacity to rise above the setbacks and to make a gallant effort to "press toward the mark of the high calling of God." His story is especially compelling for those who are engaged in formal ministry, and those who are serious about their personal walk of faith. Preparing for and Experiencing the Challenges of Leadership emerges from life experience, attempting the untried, experimenting in business, taking advantage of opportunities, sometimes failing, always landing on his feet, climbing the rungs of leadership in national organizations as prominent as the National Urban League, and as storied as the National Primitive Baptist Convention. Dr. Ernest Ferrell has made his mark as a leader. I am elated that we finally get to learn from his journey.

- Adam J. Richardson, Jr.
115th Bishop, African Methodist Episcopal Church
Florida and the Commonwealth of the Bahamas

FOREWORD
BY
Marc H. Morial

"Preparing for and Experiencing the the Challenges of Leadership"

Preparing for the Challenges of Leadership resonates with me in many profound ways. It is not easy, nor is it glamorous as some may believe. As Ferrell's book outlines, it involves many ups and downs, successes, failures, triumphs and tragedies.

Being an effective leader is an extremely difficult and demanding challenge, Reverend Ernest Ferrell is such a leader. At the National Urban League we have considered him to be our spiritual link. He continues to lead the prayers at Urban League meetings, including family sessions, delegate assemblies, luncheons and the like. His commitment to his faith, and that faith is a motivating factor in his work on behalf of the people of the Tallahassee community, is well known and highly respected.

I will always be grateful to Reverend Ferrell for the authorship of a National Urban League song that he not only composed, but sung, and that has stirred the heart of the Urban League Movement on many occasions. The song tells the complete story of the Movement, and continues to be used by many of our local Affiliates across the nation at board trainings and community meetings.

Preparing for and Experiencing the Challenges of Leadership tells Reverend Ernest Ferrell's story and contains lessons that I not only relate to, but have been a part of as legislator, Mayor, and now as President of the National Urban League.

I offer my congratulations to my friend Ernest Ferrell on behalf of the National Urban League.

Marc H. Morial,
President and Chief Executive Officer,
National Urban League

Contents

About My Father 16

About My Mother 18

Acknowledgements 21

Introduction 30

Tried to Kill a Fly 34

How I Skipped First and Fourth Grades 35

Close Encounter With a Rat 38

Basketball Championship
    at Barrow Hill Junior High School 40

Missed Opportunity To Meet
    Dr. Martin Luther King Jr. 42

Summer Vacation in Miami, Florida 44

Migrant Workers in Waterville, New York 46

The First Black Cashier 50

Military Tour of Duty 54

Outburst at an Integrated Theater 57

Internship at Federal Correctional Institution 59

Graduated from Florida A&M University 61

A Challenge in Perry, Florida 66

Counseling a Fugitive 69

The Funeral of an Inmate 71

The Dangers of Stalkers 73

Called to Preach 82

Pastoral Leadership 83

First Church Pastored. 85

Second Visionary Experience 92

The Second Church. 94

What is a Primitive Baptist? 99

Elevation Through the Ranks of the Florida
State Primitive Baptist Convention 103

The Florida State Primitive
Convention Sessions Begin 110

The National Primitive Baptist
Convention, USA, Incorporated Elected President . . 123

When Loyalty Doesn't Mean Much 136

How to Get Over Betrayal 140

Appointment to the Tallahassee Urban League
Board of Directors 144

A Prayer for President George W. Bush 147

How Do the Pastor and CEO
Complement Each Other? 150

The Urban League Song 154

Words to The Urban League Song 155

Conclusion 156

About the Author Reverend Dr. Ernest Ferrell. 158

Dedicated to
My Loving Parents the Late
Robert Ferrell Sr.
And
Hallie Vaughn Ferrell

*"Thank God for you
your family loves you"*

About My Father

I did not have a long relationship with my father because he died when I was only ten years old; however, the time that I did have with him was very special. My father was a very hard-working man who took care of his family in the old traditional way. He brought home the bacon, so to speak, and my mother cooked and took care of the family.

I remember when our family had food and, others in the community did not have food to feed their families, we would all share and help out whenever we could. Our house was always a place where everyone would come when storms blew up in the area, we would share a bed or pallet on the floor. Whatever it took to accommodate, we did it without a fuss. No one was ever turned away.

My father was not the disciplinary in the family, he mostly left that up to my mother; however, he did not have to be the disciplinary because we knew not to cross the line with him. All he had to do was just look at us and we would fall in line, and our mother would use that when she had a problem with us. She would say: "Alright now, I'm going to tell your father when he comes from work." We would calm down immediately because we knew our father did not play.

The thing that I remember most about my father was him being very particular about his tools, mainly because his occupation was, by trade, called a "paint and body man." He painted and repaired wrecked cars, which meant that his tools were essential to his work, which kept his family fed and clothed.

One day he was looking for his hammer; it was not where he kept it. He asked his boys about the hammer. "Where is my hammer?" When we did not have the right answer, he gave us an ultimatum. He said, When I wake up in the morning, my hammer better be found." We were afraid of what he would do if his hammer was not found.

This was one of the those times we all began to pray, at least I knew I did. I said, Lord, we need your help. None of us knew where the hammer was, and we don't need our father to wake up in the morning before he goes to work without his hammer, so please, Lord, we need your help.

The Lord works in mysterious ways and early the next morning the Lord answered our prayers. My brother James said that he dreamed the hammer was in a certain drawer in the house, and when we opened that drawer, the hammer that was lost was now found, miraculously found, and all of our butts were spared. I thanked the Lord for my brothers' dream.

And then there was another situation about my father that I will always remember. Where we grew up the land we lived on was full of pecan trees, and every year about the same time, when the County Fair was coming to town, the pecan trees would be loaded with pecans. It seemed that the storm would always come and blow down the pecans the same time every year, and we looked forward to picking them up because it meant that we would have funds to go to the fair.

On this particular night, the storm came at the right time, the wind blew, but something happened during the night. We all heard noises which sounded like someone was trying to break into the house; it was very disturbing and woke all of us up, and we were afraid of what was happening on the outside.

Well, my father took as much of this as he could, so he took his gun and he was going to confront whatever it was outside, but my mother insisted that he not go outside. He listened for a while until he just could not take it anymore. The noise continued, my father went outside and opened fire on the tree where he thought the sound was coming from. The sound seemed to have gotten worse, so he fired again and again until finally he braved the wind and the rain only to find out it was a raincoat stuck around the tree. Every time the wind blew, the raincoat would flap around the tree over and over; my father removed the raincoat and with some silent laughter, we all went back to bed.

The next thing I remembered about my father was him getting very sick, we were told they took him to Thomasville, Georgia, to a hospital. He had heart problems.

Many times when he was in pain and discomfort, he would always ask me to rub his back because he said that my hands would help him sleep. I always looked forward to rubbing my father's back. When he left for the hospital, he never came back alive. I heard the bell in the Mt. Olive Missionary Baptist Church ring out, which was a sign that someone in the community had died, that time it was my father.

About My Mother

My mother, Hallie Vaughn Ferrell, was the disciplinary in the house. She always seemed to be having babies, long before I knew where babies came from. I observed that every time my mother went into a certain room in our house, along with another woman, when they came out, I had a brother. As a young child, I thought that was a miraculous room, because before they went in that special room, I was the baby; when they came out, I no longer was the baby, I was now the "knee" baby.

A year before my father died, my mother and that same lady went into that particular room, when they came out, I had another brother which moved me further down the chain of command.

My mother was the most compassionate, loving mother that anyone could have. She loved all of her children, sons and her daughters. And when my father died, she had to become the mother and the father of the house. For many years after my father died, my mother was lost in that position because my father did everything in running the house, my mother was too busy being a good house wife.

My older brother assumed some of the responsibilities by becoming a father figure. He was only twenty-two years old himself with a wife and two young sons. That was very taxing for my mother. I must admit, my mother spoiled me because I was much like her. While my older sister was married and away, my other sister was at the end of her teenage years trying to live her life, my other brothers were all teenagers doing their thing, I was always close, available, looking out for my mother's needs. We had a close bond. She loved all of her children, but she knew that she could always count on me. When she was sick, I was there for her. She would call on Ernest and I would always answer her call, no matter what.

One of the proudest days of her life was when I accepted Jesus Christ as my Savior at six years old. She asked me, "How long are you going to keep him?" I said, all of my life and to this day I have kept my promise. There were so many special moments I had with my mother. When I told her that God had called me to preach, she was so proud of me. I remember when she was declining in health and her body was deteriorating more and more each day. I found myself having to do some very difficult things for her as a son. One day she was having difficulties in bathing herself and asked me for help. It was very embarrassing for her and me, but I did what I had to do and she thanked me.

My mother had a great sense of humor. Each day I would take my mother to day care where seniors would stay during the day. This particular day I was about ten minutes late picking her up, she got into the car with a solemn look on her face, she said, "Son, you were late today to pick me up. You dropped me off in September and, look, its October now! What's wrong with you?" Then we paused and we both started laughing. My mother was declining from dialysis three times a week for over three years. Her arms were overworked from the ports used. And every time she went for treatment it hurt me as much as it hurt her, but she was content. It was like a baby when it cries and you don't know what to do. They cannot tell you what's wrong, so there is very little you can do to stop the pain that occurs over and over. I knew that one day she'd be gone and I would not cry because I knew she would not have to go through dialysis ever again.

She would be at peace with God, and I would be at peace with God as well. I knew she would be in a much better place. When it came time to eulogize my mother, her pastor was not available; and

I asked God to give me the strength to eulogize my mother. I will never forget, that eulogizing my mother was a tough thing for me to do, but God was with me. He gave me the strength that I needed, I spoke from the scriptures that best described my mother: Matthew 5:9, "Blessed are the peacemakers for they shall be called the children of God." My mother was a peacemaker; she was a faithful child of God. She loved her family and everyone else. Before she died, she started having a special day set aside for her family. She could not buy gifts for all of us during Christmas, so she cooked all of our favorite foods instead. After she passed, we continued the tradition in memory of her.

Acknowledgements

When I was a young boy growing up in Tallahassee, Florida, we lived in what we called the country, located about five miles past the city limits. I was too young to even consider myself smart or highly educated. I barely finished high school, so I never thought of having a glass ceiling breakthrough, I did not know what that really meant at that time. I did think that I would be a great singer because I wanted to sing, like Nat King Cole, Brooke Benton, and Sam Cook whom I considered to be real singers. The low expectation that I had of myself was completely different from what so many others thought of me. Without the positive things that many people believed in me, I really don't know where I would be today or where my many challenges would have led me. So I really do thank all of my supporters over the years for the impact they had on me, some good, some bad or indifference, but they all mattered and help me become who I am today.

Many people influenced my life over these 71 years. First and foremost were, my mother and my father. My mother saw in me a gift from God bundled up with love and compassion for others, and she often rewarded me with special gifts, one in particular was my very first bicycle, when no one else in the family or even in the neighborhood had one. My father saw in me a hand of healing and comfort. Whenever his back was hurting from his congestive heart problems, he would always call on me to rub his back. I was only about six years old, but until his death four years later, I was always there for him.

Others included my fifth grade teacher, Mrs. Young, who saw in me great potential, as she made me read and write (more than I would have done on my own). Then there was my basketball coach and principal, Mr. Wallace H. Burgess. He believed in me and saw a talent for basketball, which resulted in our basketball team winning the junior high school district championship. Our team won over, what was called "those old men from the city schools." The good others saw in me continued. A stranger, at the time I was a bag boy at the local Winn Dixie Store, saw in me great potential from how I was motivated by his tip for carrying his groceries to his car, he gave me a quarter. A quarter in 1963 was a big deal, but more important he gave me great conversation. Little did he know how much the quarter, and the conversation would influence me. From that tip and conversation, for over 50 years he became a friend and an influence that I'll always remember. He was a local attorney, Leonard Pepper.

The late Mr. Freeman Lawrence, my high school principal saw in me character and talent. One afternoon after school was out, several of my singing friends and I were practicing in the school auditorium without permission. We were really in high gear when Principal Lawrence heard our singing and came to see what was going on. Of course we were into our singing and did not hear him coming. We were shocked as he called our names, "What are you boys doing in here without permission?" We had no good explanation and said we were sorry. Mr. Lawrence asked us, "Are you boys in the Glee Club? " No, sir, we responded. "Well, you are now. I want all of you to report to Mrs. Polly Anna Lawrence tomorrow and join the Glee Club."

These were only a few of the many examples of what others saw in me that I did not see in myself. The list goes on and on, including the late Reverend G. W. Hill, my pastor at the time, I accepted the call to preach the Gospel of Jesus Christ at a young age (21 years old). Reverend Hill did not follow the usual protocol for young ministers just beginning to preach. They would always have to preach on the floor before they could preach from the pulpit. Reverend Hill saw in me great potential and I was allowed to preach from the pulpit. His confidence in me went even further. Occasionally, when he did not feel up to it, he would ask me, "Do you have a word from the Lord today?" Reverend Hill believed deeply in the scriptures which teach that we should always be ready. My answer to him was, "Yes sir, I am ready."

Throughout this book, you will experience what the Lord has blessed me to achieve from the support of those who saw in me things that I did not see in myself. The result has been a strong force in my life that helped me prepare for the many challenges of leadership that I have had over the years.

I give thanks to my friends, family, well-wishers, and above all, to God, who made me in his image and likeness and breathed into my nostrils the breath of life. From those experiences, I have been able to pastor two successful churches, serve as President of the Florida State Primitive Baptist Convention, with hundreds of churches and thousands of members. I have served as President of the National Primitive Baptist Convention with churches in 18 states with thousands of members. I have served as President and CEO of the Tallahassee Urban League, provided assistance to over 30,000 individuals and families; graduated from Florida A & M University with a BS degree in sociology and a minor in correction. These are only a few of the many accomplishments that I have achieved thanks to the people, the institution, family and friends which got me to where I am today. I give all the glory to God for what he has done for me.

I thank my wife, Mary, who has been there for me over 50 years. She continues to be all that I need and has supported me from the very beginning. I thank the members of my very first church family, Galilee Primitive Baptist Church, and the members of the St. Mary Primitive Baptist Church where I am currently serving. A special thanks to the Tallahassee Urban League family for over 44 years we have served well over 30,000 families and individuals throughout the Tallahassee and surrounding communities. They thought enough of me to name The Tallahassee Urban League Office Building in my honor The Ernest Ferrell Building.

Finally, I want to thank the National Urban League movement for the experience and the recognition that I have received from the last four presidents and CEOs, Vernon E. Jordan, Jr., John E. Jacobs, Hugh B. Price, and now Marc H. Morial current President. I have truly been a blessed man over the years with so many friends and family. I am grateful and blessed in one way or another from each of you listed on the next pages. You are a part of my many experiences and my challenges.

The persons listed below, in one way or another, have had an impact on me during my experiences in preparing for the challenges of leadership.

Ralph D. Abernathy
Anita Abrams
Benjamin Adams
Curtis Adams
Danny Adams
Gracie Adams
Julia Wynn Adams
LeMoyne Adams
Marjorie Adams
Minnie Adams
Roosevelt Adams
Samuel Adams
Sheryl Adams
Benjamin Adams
Adewale Adewumi
David Albritton
Irma R. Albritton
Livingston Albritton, II
Livingston Albritton, III
Livingston Albritton, Sr.
Lucille Alexander
Virginia Alexander
Felton Alexander
Herbert Alexander
Sarah Allen
Caesar Allen
Remus Allen
Ruby Allen
James Ammons
Alice Anderson
Fairfield Anderson
Gladys Anderson
Joephine Anderson
Lewis Anderson
Oretha Anderson
R. L. Anderson
Wash L. Anderson
Gayle Andrews
Ruth B. Armstrong
Frazier Arnold

Elizabeth Ash
Dubose Ausley
Loranne Ausley
Debra Austin
Doris Austin
Elkin Austin
James Austin
Larry Austin
Parthenia Austin
Puretha H. Austin
Elizabeth Baker
Mary Baker
Mary A. Baker
Edith Willis Banks
Early Banks
Harry Banks
James A. Barge
James Barnes
Helena Barrington
Kenneth Barrington
Ethel Bass
Burney Battle
Carl Batts
Harold Batts
Germaine Smith Baugh
James Beck
Lillie F. Berry
Barbara Billingslea
Valerie Bivins
Virgil Bivins
Carl Blackman
Kristen C. Blackman
Lynn Blackman
Lester Blackshear
Lillie Ruth Blackshear
Louise Blackwell
George Bland
Derrick Blathers
Alice M. Boggs
Stephanie Bowden

Lue Anna Bowens
Spencer Bowens
Ron Bradford
Karla Bradley
Bernice Bradley
Emanuel Bradley
Isaiah Bradley
Jacob Bradley
Oscar Bradley
Rosa Bradley
Samuel Bradley
Veronica Bradley
Samuel Bradley, Jr.
Samuel Bradley, Sr.
Walter M. Brame
Charles Brannon
Lillian Brantley
Mary Bridgewell
Bernice Britt
Beverly Brooks
David Brooks
Sylvia Brooks
Betty Brown
Bobby Brown
Charles Brown
Chester Brown
Clanzel Brown
Josephine J. Brown
Lorraine Brown
Queen Brown
Raymond Brown
Sherwood Brown
Thomas Brown
Thomas Brown
Annie M. Browning
Thaddeus Bruce
Victoria Bruce
Johnnie Bruce
Yale Bruce
Elaine Bryant

Rosa Bryant
Robert Bryant, Sr.
Robert Bryant, Sr.
Laraine E. Bryson
Edward Buckner
James A. Buford
Lillie Buggs
Willie Buggs
Joe Bullard
Ruby Burgess
Victoria Burgess
Wallace H. Burgess
Chris A. Burney
Ester Bush
Carolyn K. Butler
Maggie Lewis Butler
Bob Butterworth
Ralph Cain
Shirley Cain
Larry Campbell
Norma Campbell
Mary B. Carnegie
Lenedra A. Carroll
Ann Carter
Louis Chambers
Yvonne Chambers
Jerry Chance
Lattamore Chavis
Comer Cherry
James Chester
John Christie
Mattie Cisrow
Charlie C. Clark
Louis Clark
William B. Clark
Bennie Clary
Harry Cloud, Sr.
Cardelea Cobbins
J. O. Coldwell
Althamese Collins
Doris Collins
Moses Collins
Sip Collins
Sylvia Collins
Joe Colson
Juanita S. Colson

Kate Condra
Maudine Cooper
Tommie L. Cooper
Ethel Costin
Z. D. Coston
Denise Cotman
Gwendolena R. Cox
Kerrick Cox
Jerry Crawford
Robert Crocker
Benjamin Crump
Minnie B. Crump
Jeraldine Cubbins
Carolyn Davis Cummings
Dan Cunningham
Andy Curro
Richard Danford
Richard Danford, Jr.
Darrell Daniel
Euzera Daniels
Tommie C. Daniels
DeSilva Davis
Anita L. Davis
Percy Davis
Robert Davis
Mitchell Dawkins
George Dean
Carolyn C. Demps
Flossie Denmark
Alfred Dennis
Vitalis Dennis
D. H. Dillon
Laura Dixie
Lari Dixie
Roosevelt Dixon
V. J. Donaldson
Viola Douglas
Ed Duffie, Jr.
Myles Duggans
Julia Duke
Kenneth Duke
Alice Dupont
Bobby Duval
Regina Earls
Robert Emanuel
David Eummer

T. Willard Fair
John Feagin
Ronnie Ferguson
Rudolph Ferguson
Henrietta Ferrell
Audrey Ferrell
Clarence Ferrell
Elbert Ferrell
Frances A. Ferrell
James Ferrell
Leroy "Stoney" Ferrell
Ralph Ferrell
Wesley Ferrell
Wilaford Ferrell
Wilbert Ferrell
Anika Fields
Ernest Fields
Henry Finley
Alice Fisher
Grace B. Fitz
Johnny Fitz
J. Lucious Fitzgerald
Joyce Fitzgerald
Lillie D. Fleming
Carrie Flowers
Fred Flowers
Kenton Floyd
W. A. Floyd
Ann Forbes-Jones
Lonnie J. Ford
Alvin J. Ford
James R. Ford
Lonnie D. Ford
Terrance Ford
William Foster
Terry Fresley
James Frison
Mary Gaines
Robert Gaines
Roland Gaines
Raymond Gaines, Sr.
Betty Gainous
Ruth Gainous
Sara Garcia Timothy
  Gainous
O. G. Galloway

John T. Gassaway
Leslie D. Gay
Anne Richardson Gayle-
    Felton
Clara Floyd Gaymon
Jeremiah Gee
Eloise Gentry
Theodis Gillespie
Geneva Gilliam
Israel Givens
William T. Gladys
Devurn Glenn
Cheryl Gonzalez
Henry Gordon
Billy Graham
Carol Graham
Eddie Graham
Lee Graham
Willie Graham
Susan Grant
Elaine Green
John Green
Ray Green
Albert Green, Jr.
Frances Green, Jr.
Robert Greenberg
Sandra O. Gregg
Beulah Gregory
Linn Ann Griffin
Annie C. Hailstock
Brewer Hall
Mary Hall
Everline H. Hamm
Michael Hannah
Nettie Harrell
Betty Harris
Dorothy Harris
Early Harris
John D. Harris
Lee Harris
Roosevelt Harris
Mose Harrison
Leanders Harvey
Bill Haskin
Joseph Hatchett
Jessie Hawkins

Isaac Hayes
Lorenzo Hayes
Richard D. Hayes
Samuel Hayes
Sarah Hayward
Bernice Henderson
David Henderson
Gloria Henderson
J. Howard Henderson
Linda Henderson
Lucille Henderson
Marvin Henderson
Robert Henderson
Charles Hendley
J. R. Hendley
Mae Hendley
Brenda Henry
Israel Henry
Clarence Herring
Eddie Hill
Rosalie Hill
Ann J. Hinson
Prince Hinson, Jr.
Prince Hinson, Sr.
Vivian Hobbs
L. V. Hobbs
Katherine Hoffman
Dilcy Hogan
Elson Hogan
Faye Hogan
Freddie Hogan
George Holiday
R. B. Holmes
Maggie Hordge
Maggie Hordge
Willie B. Horton
Jane Houle
Rosa Houston
Sarah Houston
Doris Howard
R. H. Howard
Corey Howse
James Hudson
Marilyn Hudson
James Humose
Johnnye Humphrey

Henry C. Hunter
Michael Imparato
R. B. Ivory
Mamie Jackson
Michael Jackson
Eddie Jackson
Elaine S. Jackson
Jerrlyne Jackson
Linda Jackson
John E. Jacob
Malinda J. James
Lewis Jefferson
Norman Jefferson
Studson Jefferson
Annie Jerger
Stephanie Jerger
Thelma Johnson
Augusta Johnson
Eugene Johnson
Freddie Johnson
Josarah Johnson
Leroy Johnson
Nellie P. Johnson
Betty Jones
Carrie Mae Jones
Judy Jones
Willie Jones
Jerome Jones
Johnnie M. Jones
Margaret Jones
Margaret M. Jones
P. L. Jones
Vernon E. Jordan
Carrie Judge
W. D. Judge
Anthony Jugger
Valerie Jugger
Samuel Jugger
Leonard Kelly
J. Harvey Kerns
Jackie Kilpatrick
Jessena Kilpatrick
Marie Kilpatrick
S. P. Kilpatrick
Darryl King
Emily King

Jessie King
Maggie King
Melba King
Costa Kittle
Emma Kittle
Dan Kleman
Gladys Knight
Tammy Knight
Samuel Knight
Harold Knowles
Pattie Labelle
O. Sylvia Lamar
Eugene Lamb
Joseph Landers, Jr.
Dale Landry
Lisa Lang
Velma W. Larkins
Lonya S. Lawrence
Callie C. Lawrence
Darrell Lawrence
Freeman D. Lawrence
Joseph Lawrence
Polly Anna Lawrence
Thelma Lawrence
Lois Lawson
Alfred Lawson, Jr.
Arthur Lawson, Jr.
Carol Lawyer
Catherine Lawyer
Esther Leach
Clemson Leach
Fred Lee
Daniel Leon
George Lewis, III
Henry Lewis, III
Minnie Likely
Joanna Hudson Little
Florine W. Littles
F. L. Livingston
Forrest E. Livingston
Richard Lloyd
Abraham Lofton
Warren E. Logan, Jr.
Willie Lomack
Byron Long
Elijah Lucas

Gwen Lucas
Henry Lyons
Timothy Lyons
Dorothy Maddox
Betty Madison
Evelyn Madison
Loretta Malone
Eva Manning
Ida Manning
Jane Marks
John Marks, III
Mae Marshall
Edwina B. Martin
Evelyn B. Martin
Richard Mathews, Sr.
Tawanna Maxwell
Isaac V. Mayes
Patricia Mayes
Willie Mayes
Ingrid Maysonette
Julius McAllister, Jr.
Gloria McBride
Markeith McCarthy
Catherie McClary
Bessie Mae McClendon
Freddie G. McClendon
Louis McClendon
Lester McClyde, Jr.
Al McCoy
Brenda W. McDuffie
Calvin McFadden
Carolyn McGriff
James T. McLawhorn, Jr.
Jackie McMillan
Benji McMiller
Spurgeon McWilliams
Columbia Meeks
Lee Etta Meeks
Lee Walter Meeks
Olivia Meeks
Perker Meeks
Michelle Melton
Keith Miles
Moses G. Miles
Willie M. Miles
James Miller

Dorothy Millines
Patricia Mims
Donald Mitchell
Evelyn Joy Mitchell
Ronald Mitchell
W. L. Mitchell
Bill Montford
Oscar Montgomery
Jacques Moody
Andre Moore
Yvonne Moore
Edna R. Moore
Emma Moore
George Moore
Michael Moore
Shelia Moore
Alverta Morris
Nancy Morris
Tempie Morris
Mose Mosley
Lottie Muldrow
William Muldrow
Aurielle Neal
Christopher Neal
Ingrid Neal
Jamaal Neal
Kevin Neal
Nija Neal
Althea R. Neal
R. L. Neal
Charles Neal, Jr.
Charles Neal, Sr.
Phillip J. Nelson
Phyllis Y. Nichols
Zebedee Nicholson
Edwin Norwood, Jr.
James Oliver
Florida Parker
Eva Parker
Gwendolyn O. Parker
Herbert G. Parker
Lewis Parker
Darryl Parks
Diane Patterson
Patsy B. Payne
Alice Peacock

Porter G. Peeples, Sr.
Ernest Pender
Clara Penny
Theodore Penny
Michael Penny
Leonard Pepper
Aubrey Perry
Benjamin L. Perry, Jr.
Bobby Phills
Gilda Phills
Carlton Philpot
Mary Pipes
Vivian Pope
Wanda Poppell
Christal R. Powell
Errin Powell
James Powell
Erroll Powell
Hugh Price
Terry Price
Irvin Pride
Gladys Proctor
LaMichael Proctor
Ruth Proctor
Tyrone Proctor
William Proctor
George Proctor, Jr.
George Proctor, Sr.
Jerome Pye
Wayne Rachal
Sandra Rackley
Sherrill Ragans
Lottie Ragland
Jeffrey Rainey
Eddie Randolph
Martha Randolph
Tamera Reese
Mary Reid
Stanley Reid
Carl Rhodes
Whipple Richard
C. E. Richardson
Connie Richardson
A. J. Richardson
Curtis Richardson
Edgar Richardson

Emma Richardson
Fannie A. Richardson
Frankie Richardson
John Richardson
Karla Richardson
Johnny Richardson, II
Johnny Richardson, Sr.
Derryck Richardson, Sr.
Benjamin K. Richmond
Lillie Mae Ricks
Mary Rivers
R. T. Rivers
Doc Roberts
Shirley F. Roberts
Gail Robinson
Nathaniel Robinson
Dinsimore Robinson
Eddie Robinson
Josephine Robinson
Larry Robinson
Leola Robinson
Melvin Robinson, Jr.
Annette Rogers
Joyce Rolle
Reginald Rolle
Ezekiel Rollins
Major E. Rollins
Nolan Rollins
Frank Ruch
Ben Ruff
Frank Rush
Ronnie Russell
Dorothy Sampson
Huet Sampson
Juanita Samuels
Thomas W. Samuels
Raymond Sanders
Teresa Sanders
William Sanders
Alberta Sapp
Sharon Saunders
Thomas Scott
Delores Scott
Eunice B. Scott
Randolph Scott
Vincent L. Shannon

Bobbie Sheffield
Pelita Sheffield
James Shelby
Donald Sheppard
Audrey Shine
Roxie Shine
Jacquelyn Shuler
Betty Simmons
James Simmons
Jimmy Simmons
O. Jermaine Simmons
Angeletta Sloan
Angela Smith
Brenda R. Smith
Jenee Smith
Sammie Smith
Betty Smith
Carl Smith
Charles U. Smith
Clinton H. Smith
Owen Smith
Walter C. Smith
Cornelius Speed
Michelle Spence
Charles Stafford
Frances Stafford
Francis Stallworth
Theotis Stallworth
Vivian Stallworth
Evelyn Stanley
Terry Steaple
C. K. Steele
Bettye Stevens
Billy Stevens
Charles Stevens
Phelicia Stiell
James Strickland
Doris Swain
Mack Swain
Mildred Swearingen
J. R. Swilley
Patrica Tankerson
Larry Tatum
Aretha Taylor
Jerome Taylor
Johnnie B. Taylor

Alfred Taylor
Bee Taylor
Curtis Taylor
James Taylor
Samuel Taylor
Ella S. Teal
Clarence Thomas
Gwen Thomas
Kimball Thomas
Laughton D. Thomas
Henry M. Thomas, III
Anita Favor Thompson
Arther Thompson
Charles Thompson
Gerri Thompson
Leroy Thompson
Luetta Thompson
Renson Thompson
Rutha Thompson
Theodore Thompson
Tina Thompson
Valerie Thompson
Anthonty Thurston
Minnie Tolliver
Alma Tooley
Madelyn Towels
Ernest Tucker
Beverly Urgent
Curtis Vaughn
Marion Wade
Elouise Walker
Stanley L. Walker
Willie F. Walker
Shadrick Walker, Sr.
Eva C. Wanton

Stella Ward
Doc Ward, Jr.
Victoria Warner
Clarence Warren
Collette Warren
Darren Warren
David Washington
Arthur Washington
Florence Washington
Naomi Washington
Penney Washington
Samuel Washington, Jr.
Elnora Watson
Ester Watson
Rosetta D. Waymon
Willie J. Weatherspoon
Joseph Webster
Julian White
Lossie W. White
Robert White, Jr.
L. Yvonne Whitehead
Kimberly William
Albert Williams Sr.
Albert Williams Jr.
Cecil Williams
Daisy B. Williams
Emma B. Williams
Patricia Williams
J. T. Williams
Kay S. Williams
Curtis Williams
Daisy Williams
Ella Williams
Frank Williams
Joe Williams

Marjorie Williams
Millard C. Williams
Mozella Williams
Noah Williams
Roscoe Williams
Thorton Williams
Willie Williams
Willie J. Williams
Charlie Williams, Jr.
Beatrice H. Wilson
George Wilson
Gladys L. Wilson
Lucian Wilson
Corker Wimberly
Mable Wimberly
Amanda Winn
Bernice Wise
Matthew Woody
Betty Woolfork
Robert Woolfork
Fred Wright
Joseph Wright
Julia Mae Wynn
Isaiah Yant
Pearl Yant
Vonda Yates
Bernard Yates
Jonathon Yates
Maynard Yates
Maynard Yates, Jr.
Mattie Young
Shirley Ziegler
Lincoln High 62

INTRODUCTION

This book, has been in the makings for over ten years. Finding the time and the inspiration to write it has been a real test for me. I realized that my time on this side of the grave is limited, which motivated me to get in a hurry and begin writing. I believe that it would be a tragedy and an inexcusable shame for me not to share my experiences with the world on what shaped my life so that others could see how God's goodness and mercy sustained me through all of the challenges which helped me to finish this book.

My life journey has brought me this far. Thank you, Lord for all you have done.

When you read this book, you will see and understand how the Lord spared my life from so many situations starting with my brother Wilbert innocent show of love for me while he tried to kill flies on a cheesecloth that covered me while I was in my baby crib. He thought he was protecting me from the flies but, little did he know the same spray which protected me from the flies, if sprayed directly over me, it could also kill me. When I tried to walk off the back of a moving truck into the path of oncoming traffic on our way to pick beans in Watersville, New York, I began to realize that the Lord really wanted me.

Because I was afraid of my first grade teacher, each morning when I arrived at school, I skipped my first grade class and went to my big sister Shirley's class. Each morning my first grade teacher would come by, catch me by my hand, and switch me all the way back to her class (paddle or whip).

All of those whippings were getting me prepared for the many challenges that I would face for years to come. My preparation for leadership continued to develop, and my challenges continued to grow. Each year I learned more and more and continued to develop.

One critically important thing that I learned, was when the Lord chose me to preach the Gospel, he prepared me for the long haul. God did not call me to leave me alone, but to fulfill the promises of His

Word with me and never leave me alone. My life experience expressed in this book were no accidents.

When I escaped from a man wielding a knife against another man in the restaurant where I worked during a summer job. God's grace and mercy continued to protect me, guide me and lead me because he knew that I would need all of the training, all of the experiences necessary to protect me. When my brother, cousin and I went to pick beans in Watersville, New York, God protected me yet another time.

There's an old saying that the Lord looks out for babies and fools. It's really true because we were truly fools.

On that same trip while we were in Watersville, we also did some other crazy things. On the weekends we would go down to the river banks and run our hands under the banks and pull out fish one at a time until we got as many as we wanted.

Throughout this book, you will experience with me how the Lord protected me so that I would be able to continue on my long journey, preparing me for the leadership which was yet to come. So many ups and so many downs, so many hills and valleys came my way, but they were never too hard for God, through his divine will, He always brought me through.

Case in point, when I got my very first car from a man that I used to work for cutting his grass during the summer. He sold me the car for less than a hundred dollars. It was the most beautiful car that I had ever seen on the inside.

I tried everything that I could to destroy it. Driving fast around dangerous curves, rough roads, through hazardous conditions. And the Lord's security forces continued to protect me. The Lord spared me so that I would be able to tell this story. To God I give the glory.

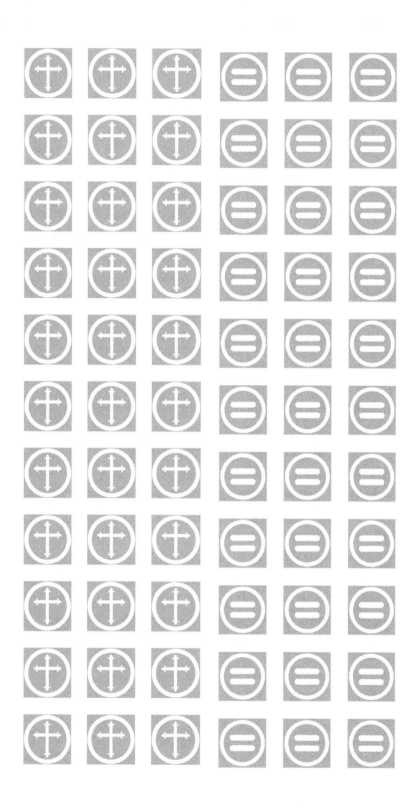

LET THE

CHALLENGES

BEGIN

Edited by
Dr. Jerrlyne Jackson

Tried to Kill a Fly

According to my mother and sister when I was a baby I had a life changing experience that had long term impact on whether or not I would survive to fulfill my preparation of leadership.

It all started when I was asleep in my homemade baby crib. The crib was draped with cheese cloth, to cover me from flies, that lit on the cheese cloth, but was unable to get to me, in the crib.

This was an acceptable practice that many families would use back in the days when there was no air-conditioning for our family. My mother would use the cheese cloth as she worked in the house cleaning and making sure that everything was just right.

My brother observed my mother when she saw flies on the crib. She would get the spray gun and spray the flies, the flies would fall dead, sweep them up and put them in the trash. This was routine on any given day.

On this particular day my brother would try his hand at killing some flies. So he got the spray gun, saw the flies lighting on the cheese cloth covering me as I slept. My brother followed what he thought was doing the right thing. He took the spray gun and began spraying the flies on the cheese cloth, not knowing that what he was doing would kill the flies and the baby, which was me.

My brother was only a year and-a-half old, so he was excited about killing flies off of his baby brother. His baby brother was on his way to heaven while he was excited. My mother finally observed what was going on. She picked up my limber body, took me outside so that I could breathe and get fresh air.

The quick thinking from my mother's actions saved my life, resulting in the beginning of my long journey preparing me for the challenges of leadership. From that day forward, my mother put the spray gun out of reach from my brother and others who did not know the difference from killing flies and killing her babies. Thank you, mom, for saving your child.

How I Skipped First and Fourth Grades

When it was time for me to begin school at the age of six years old, I remember the first day that I arrived at Rainey Elementary School with my sister, Shirley.

I skipped my first grade class and went directly to her class. When I saw my first grade teacher, who looked so white that I was afraid of her and my fear grew even more when she came to my sister's class to get me. She came with what seemed to me the longest and largest switch in the world.

She switched me all the way back to her classroom. Every morning the same routine: I would go to my sister's class, my teacher would come with a different switch to bring me back. This was my first experience of failure. I failed first grade because I would not stay in my class. Eventually, I passed first grade with many "butt whippings" to remember.

My second grade year was not as bad because I had a different teacher and less conflict. After my first grade extenuating circumstances, when I was just beginning to get over it, I was informed that I was going to be transferred to a new school and my new teacher was even meaner than my first grade teacher according to what others were saying.

I began to have nightmares, about moving to Barrow Hill School facing another teacher with a reputation of being mean. I will always remember how terrified I was when I arrived at Barrow Hill School. I was assigned to Mrs. Emma Douglas. Mrs. Douglas, my fourth grade teacher, that I was told was mean. It was said she would punish her students by using a car fan belt.

I was so afraid until I skipped the fourth grade. This time my sister was not there to protect me. I skipped from fourth grade to the fifth grade. The school was not that well organized so no one really questioned me about whether I was in the right class or not. At least not at the beginning of the school year.

I stayed in the fifth grade throughout most of the school year. I felt as if I belonged in the fifth grade. I was doing very well, learning a lot, and I really loved my teacher, Ms. Sarah Young. She was very helpful, especially with my reading.

It was not until the end of the school year that they discovered that I was in the wrong class and they marched me back to the fourth grade without the butt whipping that I got when I was in the first grade and moving from my sister's class back to the first grade.

However, the walk from the fifth grade back to the fourth grade seemed like an eternal walk. It seemed like I would never get to the other grade. I was devastated again. However, I did get promoted from fourth grade to the fifth grade. I only spent a few weeks in the fourth grade.

Once I adjusted to the new fifth grade, I began to develop into a different kind of student. I learned how to use my experience with mean teachers to work with teachers who had a reputation of being mean.

When I was promoted to the sixth grade my teacher was Ms. Clyde Richardson. She was a very big woman that was known to use her size and her disciplinary tools to keep her students in line. I learned from my previous experience how to save my butt, how to be nice to my teacher.

Each morning I would bring my teacher an apple or something nice. I became her favorite. She would often invite me to her home. She had two sons who were older than me and treated me like a little brother. Ms. Sarah Young and Ms. Richardson were my best experiences with teachers through the eighth grade. Ms. Young was a beautiful, engaging teacher who helped me to be the very best student that I could be.

I credit them both for the many things that I learned under their leadership. Both had a tremendous impact on me in different ways. They all helped prepare me for the ever growing challenges that I would face for years to come.

Many years later, my first grade teacher Mrs. Collette Warren became very close to me and my family. I learned that she was just trying to teach me, until her recent death, she was very special to me.

Close Encounter With a Rat

When I was growing up in what we refer to as the country, my favorite past-time was reading comic books. Once every month when the new comic book came out we would go to the grocery store and I would find the latest Superman, Spiderman and Wonder Woman, and sometime romantic books.

In one of the magazines was a picture of Bob Hope which said, draw me. I loved to draw and paint. So I responded by sending in my drawing and they responded and indicated that I had talent. I realized later that the drawing, the draw me, was just a way of getting you to buy the drawing kit.

After begging my mother for the money to pay for the kit, I ordered my draw me kit. The drawing and painting became my passion and I thought that I was good at it. My best painting was the Lord's Supper. I did not have a canvas large enough to paint the Last Supper.

So I used a wide cardboard box, opened it completely and painted the Lord's Supper on it. The result was my best work. After school I would draw and paint. Once I finished my painting I would line the walls with my art work until I ran out of space on the wall.

I decided to find some more space to store my paintings. I remember we had a crib where my father stored some of his tools and this would be a good location to store my paintings. Once I got approval from my mother I began cleaning up the other half of the crib from where my father stored his tools.

Even though my father had passed away we still maintained his tools on the other side of the crib. On the other side of the crib was corn shucks. The corn shucks pretty much were stored on the side I was getting ready to clean out to put my new found art collections. The corn shucks were cleared out, and my office was getting ready to be set up. Meanwhile, all of the rats were looking for a place to move into as well. Now that the place was cleaned, I began moving paintings into it. I was very creative. So I made my office really nicely laid out. All of the rats that were in the crib struggled for new homes while I enjoyed my new office. One day after school I was excited to get back into my new office.

While on my way to the office I observed a rat running from the crib and he was running towards me. It seemed like he was laser guided. He was coming straight towards me. I had on bell bottom pants (back in the day) and he ran directly up my pant leg, heading straight toward my family jewels.

Once he made his leap I caught him inches from making it to the jewels. I squeezed that rat until I got out of my pants, still today I don't know how exactly how that actually happened. Getting out of my pants, squeezing a rat all at the same time. I finally got out of my pants, I had squeezed that rat into potted meat. I remember the pants and the rat were both trashed and I ran into the house with just my underwear on.

From that day forward, my paintings, drawings and new office were all history. I was not taking a chance of having another rat run up my pant leg. I am not sure how this story will help me prepare for the challenges of leadership, but somewhere in this book I will be confronted with the unexpected, a close encounter with some rat-like circumstances. When I get there I will remind you of this incident.

Basketball Championship
at Barrow Hill Junior High School

From the classroom to the basketball court, my new passion was for the sport of basketball. My coach was also my principal. Mr. Freeman Lawrence, left Barrow Hill to become the principal at the original Lincoln High School. Mr. Wallace H. Burgess became my new principal and basketball coach.

We did not have very good equipment, nor did we have a good court for practice. I remember we had clay dirt courts and a goal with no nets on them. Even under those conditions, we had a great coach and a good team. I will always remember how we won most of our games over all of the rural segregated schools, which included Lake McBride, Station 1 and others in the area.

We were invited to the annual basketball tournament which was held each year in the original Lincoln High School gymnasium. We were going to have an opportunity to play against what we called "those city boys." For my teammates and I, this was like moving to the Ivy League of basketball heaven; we were going to play on the inside of a building called a gymnasium. From the clay courts to a wooden floor was unbelievable. We were all so excited until we could not sleep the night before the first tournament game.

The first game was with Griffin; we won. We also won two additional games before the championship game, which was against Bond School. Bond School was known as the best school in the city. We saw their team, and we saw how big they were at the time. And then it was our time to march onto the court with our old hand-me-down trunks and no jockey straps, I guess because we didn't know that we needed them. we were just excited to be there. It did not matter to us because we did know about them and not use to having them on.

Running up and down the court without jockey straps on raise dsome eyebrows, especially when we were flopping from side to side it was a noticeable distraction to some but we came to play ball and nothing was going to distract us from our game. The more they laughed at us, the better we played until the laughing stopped and the game was over and our team was the champion. When the dust settled, and the fact that we did not wear jockey straps and our uniforms were hand-me-downs did not matter and we were champs. I had my best game ever, we won the state championship. It was the proudest moment of our lives (my teammates and I).

Preparations for the challenges of leadership continued to develop for me. I remembered during the game, a well-known and respected coach at Lincoln High School, Coach John D. Harris said to the teams we beat: "That boy is shooting further out with one hand better than our team was shooting with two hands." That boy he was talking about was me.

We shot the lights out in that tournament, as the old saying goes. It was not until I went to high school that I learned why they laughed at our team. Nonetheless, I can laugh now; but the laughing was on them because we won the game.

Missed Opportunity To Meet
Dr. Martin Luther King, Jr.

There are many people who have marched with Dr. Martin Luther King, Jr., even those who claim to have marched with Dr. King or went to jail with him. I have not marched nor went to jail, so this story might not mean much, but the opportunity to meet with Dr. King was an overwhelming opportunity that I was selected to experience by virtue of a piece of equipment that I owned.

The word got around town that Dr. Martin Luther King, Jr., was coming to Tallahassee and that he would be meeting with local pastors of the Southern Christian Leadership Council. The meeting was going to take place at the home of the late Reverend Dr. James Hudson who lived on Gamble Street. The Leadership of SCLC, Reverend C. K. Steele, Reverend R. N. Gooden, Reverend Daniel Speed, Father David Brooks and other local pastors were invited.

This would be a historical moment and they needed to find someone to record the meeting, but no one had the proper equipment to record. This is where I came in; I was one of the few people in Tallahassee who had a recording machine. Dr. Hudson tracked me down and asked me if I would bring my tape recorder to his home and record Dr. King's message.

Tallahassee was deeply involved with civil rights and Dr. King was the leader in civil rights and his presence would be the most significant event for the local SCLC and for me. I was going to meet and record Dr. King.

The day the meeting was to take place, I arrived at Dr. Hudson's home early in time to set up and test the equipment; I made sure that everything was working just right. Once everything was set, all of the pastors were in place, we were waiting with high expectation. We were going to meet Dr. King.

After waiting for about 30 minutes we received a call from Dr. Martin Luther King, Jr.'s representative apologizing for Dr. King.

An emergency had come up and he would not be able to attend the meeting. We were all let down. No one was more disappointed than I was, but just the thought of meeting with a legend was quite fulfilling.

I cannot tell you the story that I met with Dr. King, but I came close. I can tell you as I close, that the thought of meeting with him was a great inspiration to all of us, even though we were disappointed.

Summer Vacation
in Miami, Florida

During the summer of 1961, the year before I graduated from high school, I had some exciting and challenging experiences while spending my summer vacation in Miami, Florida. My brother got me a summer job with him in one of the Morrison's Cafeterias. My job was to bust tables once the waiters completed their job. I cleaned the tables and got the dishes ready to be washed.

I lived with my Aunt Bea, as we affectionately called her. Aunt Bea babied me and spoiled me and of course I loved it very much. While living in Miami, I really appreciated the big city; and when I got paid, I would go and visit some of the sights of Miami.

I love singing, so I joined a local church and began singing in the choir. The people at the church were very friendly, and I quickly became well known and respected and loved by the members. My brother was well known in the restaurant business, and he did well for himself. I remember while working in the cafeteria I had lots of fun and there was much trash talking between the waiters and the others in the kitchen. They bragged about how much they made in tips, and laughed in a respectful way about their customers; and for the most part, it was just one big family.

However, things did get out of hand sometimes at the cafeteria, one particular day two of the kitchen staff got into a brawl. It started when these two kitchen staff workers got into a fight and began chasing each other through the restaurant. This was after the cafeteria was closed. We were all trying to stay out of their way, but they were violently fighting and throwing stuff at each other, using whatever they could get their hands on to throw. Finally, things got way out of hand when one of the men found a kitchen knife and continued after the other man chasing him around and around in the kitchen.

When he could not catch him, he threw the knife; and the man ducked, and ran out of the cafeteria. Unfortunately for me, the knife missed the intended target and hit me. The Lord protected me from the knife blade, and it turned and the butt of the knife hit me in the back of my leg. I realized much later in my life that the Lord was preparing me for much more serious situations in my life that I will be mentioning as I experience many more challenges to come.

When the knife experience was over, I knew it was time for my summer vacation to be over. Just another experience with destiny for me. After I returned to school my high school teacher, Mr. Adderly, asked all of the students in his class what we did on our summer vacation, we all shared our stories. My story was the most interesting of them all, and my preparation for the challenges of leadership continued to unfold.

Migrant Workers in
Waterville, New York

In 1956, I considered myself to be a big dreamer with much faith in God and whatever I wanted I believed the Lord would give it to me.

At 13 years old I was not old enough to get a work permit, nor a driver's permit, and not old enough to work even though I did not have a job and not old enough to drive, even though I did not have a car, but I was old enough to dream and to have faith.

In the summer of 1956, I would have an opportunity to test my faith because I wanted to go to New York to pick beans, believe it or not. Can you imagine that? The word was out that you could make lots of money and have a great time. So I wanted to go, but I was not old enough to go.

You had to be at least 14 years of age and I would not be 14 until October, and this was after school was out in June. When my mother told me that I could not go I was devastated. However, with the special relationship I had with my mother and the faith that I had in God, I prayed and told my mother that I believed that the Lord was going to make a way for me to go.

My brother and cousin was picked up by the truck, and when they left I told my mother they were going to come back for me. My mother gave me some hope. She said, "If that happened, if they come back for you I will let you go." She said that knowing the truck was not going to come back, and she knew that it was not coming back.

I laid down with my clothes on, packed and ready to go, because I was confident that that truck was coming back for me. About one hour later I heard the horn blowing and I knew that my prayers were answered, and they came back for me.

My mother could not believe what had happened. My brother and my cousin really did not want me to go, but they made room and off we went. Before it was over I realized that I should be careful what I asked for or prayed for, because in my case I got what I thought I wanted, but I got more than I really needed.

The trip to Waterville, New York was like a trip from hell. Traveling from Tallahassee, Florida, to New York, on the back of a covered truck was the most depressing thing that I had ever experienced in my life, in my young life.

This was my first and last introduction to how migrant workers lived. There is enough in this story alone to write this book. However, I will only share a few stories about the trip and how it affected me over the years and what we experienced getting to New York from Tallahassee.

I remember the benches that we sat on became so hard until my butt claimed a new identity. It became a grinding board. When I turned right, it grinded, when I turned left, it grinded, when I stood up it continued to grind. Stopping, going to the bathroom was even more humiliating.

In 1956, separate but unequal was the law of the land, and running to the woods was not a pleasant sight. I remember one day it started raining, I was watching the rain fall off the back of the truck until my eyes became fixed and I was hypnotized. I remember, uncontrollably I got up and began to walk towards the back of the truck reaching for the water.

I stepped up to the tailgate and started getting ready to walk off the truck into the oncoming traffic. Before I could step off the truck a friend reached up and pulled me back into the truck, and brought me out of my trance. What a close encounter with death that I was experiencing.

Once we finally arrived in Waterville, New York the trip from hell continued. When I saw the camp, where we would be living, the migrant reality continued. The first discouraging test was to find a decent mattress to sleep on. The best of the worse was unbelievably depressing.

After all, this camp had been used, these mattresses were used over and over each year and the camp ownership did not care about the condition. All they were concerned about was how many beans we could pick.

These mattresses were filthy and unusable. It made me appreciate what I left behind. We were not rich, but compared to where we were living, I considered us all to be rich. We made the best of what we had by taking the mattresses outside, beating them and letting the sun shine upon them for a day while we slept on the floor.

A man, wife and several children were next door to where my brother and cousin and I slept. The man was called Papa Charlie. He and his family were seasonal bean workers, and they were called "bean picking machines." They had the reputation of clearing a bean field in little time compared to all the other workers.

Papa Charlie had a big problem; he was an abuser. Every weekend after he got paid, he would keep everyone up late at night beating and abusing his wife and children. This would go on late into the night until he fell asleep. The next morning it was like nothing had happened. They would go out to the fields and work all week. The next weekend the same things were repeated—beating his wife and children. We were afraid to get involved. None of this was illegal at that time.

It did not take me long to realize that bean picking was not my greatest asset. Each day I would struggle trying to make my quota, and every day I did not do very well. At the end of the week, my paycheck was not very much, and the little I did make, the system was set up so that the camp would get most of that back in food and stuff that I really did not need.

There were some things that I did enjoy however. The camp was located in front of a really high mountain, and when we had time, we would use the mountain as a playground. We would take cardboard boxes and slide down the mountain. It was very dangerous, but we always found a way around the trees and rocks on the mountain side. We had lots of fun, and it took my mind off the bean picking for at least a while. Another pasttime that we enjoyed was fishing under the banks of the river. We would take our hands and run them under the banks of the river and pull out the fish. This was one of the most awkward and dangerous things that we did. We caught many fish, but we could have caught a snake, an eel or something else, but the Lord held true to what we had heard our mothers say, "The Lord takes care of babies and fools." We were not babies, but we truly were fools.

Remember what I told you about Papa Charlie, how he would beat his wife every Saturday night? Well, one Saturday night when the beatings stopped, we heard Papa Charlie screaming for his life. His wife finally got tired of this and took matters into her own hands. She took a hammer and broke Papa Charlie's jaw and beat him until the ambulance came and took him away.

Once the summer was over, my sister who lived in Philadelphia, Pennsylvania was going to drive up to Waterville, New York to pick my brother and I up, and we were going to catch the train back home to Florida. When my sister arrived at the camp, she was expecting us to be in good living conditions, not necessarily a summer resort, but good living conditions; however, when she arrived and saw us, she was hurt and embarrassed. She had her friend from Philly with her. We were living in a slave like migrant camp. At first, she didn't recognize who her little brothers were. She said that she was going to tell our mothers not to ever let us come to this place again. She called it something, which I won't include in the book.

Little did my sister know she did not have to tell my mother because I would never pray that prayer ever again.

The First Black Cashier

In 1962 after graduating from the Old Lincoln High School, in Tallahassee, I took a class in keypunch operation. At the time, keypunching was a highly technical skill to have for a job opportunity. A keypunch operator was the wave of the future. Little did I know at the time that my future would not be in keypunch. My first job was working at a top men's clothing store as a tailor.

The store was Alford Brothers Men Store in downtown Tallahassee. My tailoring trade from Lincoln High School paid off. I gave most of the credit to my teacher, Mrs. Aldonia Flowers, who taught tailoring. For one year, I was the tailor at Alford Brothers. It was a unique opportunity working in an all-white upscale store repairing suits and other basic tailoring needs. While working at Alford Brothers, I received a call from my high school principal, Mr. Freeman Lawrence. He said to me that he was impressed with how I conducted myself while in high school and that he believed that I would do a good job working at a local Winn Dixie Grocery Store. He said they were looking for a young man that could work his way up in their store from bag boy to store manager. I had the utmost respect for Mr. Lawrence, and if he was recommending me for a job, it would be worth me considering the job.

I immediately applied for the job and was hired. What started out as a bag boy ended up being more than I ever expected.

One day while I was carrying out my bag-boy duties and responsibilities, I noticed several well-known and respected local ministers dressed up in their ministerial pastoral attire who went straight to the manager's office and requested to see the manager. In the group was Reverend C. K. Steele, Reverend R. N. Gooden, Reverend Daniel Speed, Father David Brooks, Professor Doctor James Hudson and several other ministers of the Ministerial Alliance. They were all respected ministers and leaders of the community.

Once the manager came, they expressed concern. First and foremost, they said that the Winn Dixie Store was located in the predominantly black community, its customers were predominantly black and there were no black cashiers, they wanted that changed immediately.

The manager was Mr. Leroy Collins. Mr. Collins listened to the pastors' concern and their ultimatum, which was they wanted the Southside Winn Dixie Store to hire a black cashier and they demanded the hiring within one week. Their conversation was straight forward for the demands, making sure that their demands were met. When the week was up and Winn Dixie had ignored the ministers' demands, the Southside Winn Dixie Store was boycotted. Once the boycott began, for the next two weeks, the Southside Winn Dixie Store business dwindled to about 60% and continued to drop until it came to a virtual standstill resulting in Winn Dixie giving in to the ministers' demand. A black cashier was on the way, and that cashier was going to be me.

I was the company's choice. I had only 24 hours of training before the moment of truth came and the deadline was up and the pastors were coming to see if their demands were met. In the meantime, I was in training on the cash register. Once the pastors came in and met with the manager, they were informed that within the next 24 hours I would be working as a cashier at the Southside Winn Dixie Store. I am now in Training and was introduced to the cash register.

For me, the cash register was like a big box with numbers on it, and I had to learn how to punch in those numbers in a very short period of time to learn how to operate the cash register. On the opening day, I would be the center of attention; everyone who wanted to be a part of history lined up in my line, the first black cashier. It seems insignificant now, but in 1963 it was a big deal.

I tried not to disappoint my customers. The line of customers waiting was unbelievably long, but they patiently waited and waited and waited until all was eventually served and history had been made. I was the principal benefactor, along with the customers who waited for me to check them out. My skills started off slowly, however after several weeks I got better and better and faster and faster. Once the boycott was over, the Southside Winn Dixie Store returned to normal. The sales increased, my value to the company became more and more important. I was able to purchase stock in the company. I worked at Winn Dixie from 1963 to 1966 when I was drafted into the United States Army. After completing my two years in the Army, I went back to Winn Dixie and became the frozen food manager; I stayed there until I graduated from Florida A & M University in 1972.

Those three years I worked at Winn Dixie helped me develop my communication skills with the wonderful customers and employees that I worked with. When you work with people who are spending their money, after a while, they don't care what your color is, white or black. They develop attitudes about their hard-earned money, especially when they believe that the prices are too high and they have problems cashing their checks or when they prefer someone other than me ringing up their groceries. There was one incident in particular that I remember. Once I became proficient with the cash register and the register became a part of me, I made it into a real machine that I could run almost without looking at the keys.

On one day, a very reluctant white customer came to my line. I could tell that he really did not want to, but I was the only cashier open at the time. He placed his groceries on the counter and made me wait until all of his groceries were in place before I could start ringing up his groceries.

When I started, I rang the groceries so fast that he accused me of cheating him and asked for the manager. When the manager, Mr. Luther Collins, came and heard the man's complaint he wanted his groceries rechecked to see if I had deliberately cheated him. Mr. Collins was much slower but very efficient, and he made sure that the man watched him ring each item up.

Once the last item was finished, the total result was one penny short on the customer's side. The man was noticeably embarrassed but would not apologize. The experience and exposure I received from being the first black cashier made me somewhat of a celebrity in the community and my reputation from my success motivated me to increase my education, and brought my attention to the Civil Rights community, particularly Reverend C. K. Steele, a local icon and a nationally respected leader of the Southern Christian Leadership Conference. He represented Tallahassee as the SCLC president.

Reverend Steele encouraged me to join SCLC. I also got the attention from Florida A & M University President at the time, the late Doctor B. L. Perry, Jr., who asked me to consider serving on the Tallahassee Urban League Board of Directors as a member. From the Winn Dixie experience, my community participation began, my preparation for the challenges of leadership was leadership experience. All that I had experienced through the years was now ready to be implemented.

Military Tour of Duty

In 1966, I was drafted into the United States Army where I developed many of my leadership skills. I was very apprehensive about the military considering the fact that I was entering the Army during the war in Viet Nam and recently married.

I left Tallahassee by bus headed for the Jacksonville Intake Center. When we got off the bus in Jacksonville it was the scariest thing that I had ever experienced. We got off the bus, running as if our life was depending on it. The Sergeant In Charge made us fall in line, drop everything that we had. He was yelling like we were some wild animals.

He said, "Welcome to the United States Army." We began the induction with a physical. They lined us up against the wall, told us to drop our pants, and our underwear, while a military doctor shined a light up our butts. I was so scared until when it was time for me to pick up my underwear and put them back on, I put them on backwards.

Next we were told to turn our head, cough, while the doctor poked something into our mouths. We were examined very closely. I remember when he checked my feet I was sure that my feet would disqualify me from serving because I had overlapped toes on both feet. I was disappointed because he said, "one overlap toe, move forward."

Once the physical was over we were bused to the training barracks in Fort Benning, Georgia. Basic training at first was a real struggle for me because I did not get what I considered an important job at the time. I ended up being placed as a cook. I learned before I left home from my mother that whatever the job you have, make sure you make that job the best job you will ever have. I believe that the cook job was more of a biased position, that they meant for evil, but God made it good for me.

The cook job was good for me because when all of the soldiers were in the field I was enjoying the beauty of the truck covered with canvas that would protect me from the hot sun and the rain. While they were working up sweat, I was preparing their food. After settling down in the military, I learned how to follow orders quickly, resulting in placing me on fast track promotions.

I was promoted to E-1 out of basic training. Once I graduated from basic training I was sent to Fort Dix in New Jersey where I began advanced military training. I had some exciting experiences in the military, particularly my spiritual development in an unlikely place for that part of my life.

I had to establish myself as a soldier as well as a man of God to unlikely supporters, but I was sure that the two could work together without learning the habits of some of the soldiers. I was successful as a soldier because I received my second stripe five months into my training.

My spiritual development had a more difficult challenge to overcome. The first challenge came when I had nowhere to practice my faith. So I created my own space by placing two-foot lockers together, made a pulpit and started a Bible study on Sunday mornings. I invited other soldiers, whoever wanted to come, and a few came.

This visibility created some challenges from some of the soldiers who considered me to be just a fraud and that I was not for real and just trying to impress folks that I was all of that; and they were looking for an opportunity to prove their theory.

Soon they would get that opportunity. One day in the mess hall, where I worked and where the soldiers ate, I was on break and I was going to sit down with some of those soldiers who believed that my faith was just talk. They were going to prove that I was just a fake, so they devised a scheme.

While I was not looking one of the soldiers placed several tacks in my seat, and I sat down on them and when I sat down on those tacks they proved their point, that I was far from perfect because when I sat on those tacks my spiritual decorum left for a brief moment and I said words that I had not spoken in a very long time, words that I will not share with you in my book.

When I reacted the way I did, the soldiers thought that I was going to deny my faith because of what I said when those tacks touched my butt. Instead, I asked God to forgive me and he made me stronger in preparation for the next challenge that I would face. The results of how I handled the situation, convinced those soldiers and they became students in my Sunday school class.

The military provided me with some outstanding opportunities to serve my country and learn how to work with people of all races, cultural and ethnicities. It was while serving in Augsburg, Germany, I met an outstanding soldier named Sergeant Ernest Pender. He helped me by showing me how to lead by example.

From his leadership I was able to develop my own leadership style in how to deal fairly and considerate with the shortcoming of others. I used my God given personality to help many of my military friends. The Army proved to be the best leadership training experience that I needed to fulfill my obligation to serve my country.

The results of my tour of duty helped me realize that my preparation for leadership was now in full speed ahead. Before I completed my two years of military duty I was promoted to E-5 ranking in less than two years, which was unusual because a large number of soldiers who served for many years more did not reach that level of promotion. The military training helped me put my spiritual calling from my creator into my earthly calling for serving God's people. I am now ready to begin using my talents, gifts and wisdom from God to provide leadership to the people of God. I remember when my two years were up and it was time for me to return back home to America.

Before I could get back to Tallahassee, I landed in Washington, D. C. airport. I remember while I was waiting for my flight to Tallahassee an old white man looked at me and the other black soldiers with contempt in his eyes. He said "What are you boys doing here in D. C.?" I said, to him, "We are not boys, we are soldiers protecting people like you who don't appreciate the freedom that we are providing you each and every day." It was his statement that made me realize I was back in America, where things were changing, but not fast enough. It was a reality check for me.

Outburst at an Integrated Theater

In 1968, when I returned home from my military tour of duty in Augsburg, Germany, I was excited to get back home to be with my wife that I had been away from for two years. Tallahassee had changed tremendously.

Integration had closed down most of the black schools. Old Lincoln High School where I graduated had graduated its last class. Things were different and many changes had transpired during the two years I was away.

The Leon theater where blacks use to attend was now closed and the Florida theater where whites attended were open to everyone no matter what your color was. Now that the theater downtown was open and we could go there without any trouble, I thought I would take my wife to see a new movie that was called the Liberation of L. B. Jones.

We did not decide to go because of what was playing, because we had no idea about the Liberation of L. B. Jones, but rather we just wanted to see a movie. It just so happened on that particular night the movie showing was the Liberation of L. B. Jones. The theater was packed with mostly white patrons, and just a few blacks of which my wife and I were among the few. We were seated in the middle of the isle between most of the white crowd.

The movie started off with what appeared to be a pretty good plot, and the more it played the more intense it became. We were all at the edge of our seats. The story was about one of the richest black men in Tennessee. He was divorcing his wife for infidelity with a white police officer. The movie was based on an event that happened in a southern town where Jessie Hill Ford lived. After he wrote the book he was verbally attacked for writing about the events that had occurred in his hometown. The motion picture added to the controversy, especially a portion in the movie that really got me upset.

This wealthy black funeral home director, L.B. Jones, was at home with his family sitting on the porch, when this officer came up to the house. The officer spoke to L.B. Jones and his family in a friendly way, went into his wife's bedroom, had sex with his wife, came back out, and spoke to everybody as if nothing had happened.

That is when I exploded and shouted with a loud vigorous voice, that "C" must be out of his "D" mind, and when I said that, my wife hunched me viciously. I said it is too late, it is already out, and apparently all of the whites who were in the theater must have agreed with me because you could hear a pin drop.

As far as I was concerned, even the good plot which happened, when the man found himself in a combine machine which took his life, nothing could have maximized my feelings other than it was time for me to leave.

After the movie was over I realized what I had said could have caused a major event in the theater, but it did not. When the movie was over, my wife and I were probably the first ones out of the theater. This situation was just another way the Lord was preparing me for so many critical issues that I would be faced with in my lifetime.

Internship at a Federal Correctional Institution

Toward the end of my undergraduate degree from Florida A & M University, I was assigned to do my internship at the Federal Correctional Institution. This experience helped prepare me for the reality of institutional racism where the inmates were two blacks to one white inmate. The difference was time served. White inmates time served to black inmates time served was also extremely different based on the same crime. Punishment for blacks while serving their time was more severe than for their white counterparts.

Most of the black inmates were far less educated and it showed when they had concerns and had to express their concerns. Their concerns were expressed much differently than the white inmates. For example, the black inmates expressed themselves through real sailor cussing, kind of expressions; every other word was profanity. I really identified with them because that was who I used to be. Every word I used to say was with profanity until I learned better. The results of their cursing caused the white correctional officers to take their cursing behavior personally. Most times, the inmates with few words in their vocabulary would get more time in solitary confinement than their white counterparts.

I tried to explain to some of the more sensitive white correctional officers who would listen, that if they'd learn how to understand the frustration of many of the black inmates and show some respect, it would make their lives a lot less stressful and less confrontational; a nd many of these young inmates would spend less time in confinement.

I believe my internship really had some positive impact on both the white inmates and the black inmates as well as some of the correctional officers. I made many friends, particularly with a young white inmate who was an architect, in prison for his involvement in a blue collar crime as they called it. He and I became good friends. As a result of our friendship, he helped me design and draw the plan for a new church that we wanted to build at Galilee Primitive Baptist Church where I was serving as pastor. I'm not sure how we were able to get the drawings done while

59

my internship was being played out and he was serving time, but he was allowed to finish the drawings and I was allowed to take the plans out. The fascinating thing about that experience was I had the vision of what I wanted and he had the skills to develop my vision. Together we completed a small "masterpiece of a building" which I was told, once the church was completed by Reverend C. K. Steele, an icon in our community, he said, "The church was designed by someone who appreciated the beauty of God and designed the church as they saw God."

My internship at FCI was just another experience that helped me develop my leadership style and skills that would lead me to a continued high level of preparation for the many challenges of leadership. It was very difficult for me to go in and out of the prison each day with the heavy iron doors opening and closing. I was praying each day that I would never become an inmate in any prison system.

Although confinement and the daily possibility of danger, were not pleasant, that experience at the Correctional Institution will last me a lifetime. Especially, when I discovered from all of the inmates that a hundred percent of them were innocent and the fault was always someone else's. I treasure those moments of dialogue with the inmates because I believe that my stay at FCI not only had a positive impact on my personal development as a young man getting ready to graduate from college but also on some of the inmates that I was working with who had a change of heart from my counseling and presence. Some said that once they were released from prison they were going to do things different for the better. God gave me the wisdom and knowledge to share with the inmates, those who were willing to listen, the importance of turning their lives around and giving God a chance to help them change. It was a great joy for me to work as an intern at FCI and complete my college education in my field of study, both as a social worker and as a minister of the Gospel of Jesus Christ, fulfilling my basic theme: "We are making a difference."

As a result of my internship with FCI, I am a better man and a stronger servant of the Lord more prepared for the challenges of leadership which lay ahead for me.

Graduated from Florida A&M University

In 1968, when I returned from military duty in Augsberg, Germany, my job at Winn-Dixie was still available for me. Before I left for the Army I was a cashier at Winn-Dixie, when I returned my new job was the frozen food manager. Many of the customers remembered me and my popularity was still high.

After being encouraged by many college professors who stopped by Winn-Dixie I enrolled at Florida A&M University in 1969. I was working full time at Winn-Dixie, had recently been called to pastor the Galilee Primitive Baptist Church, and I knew if I enrolled at Florida A&M University I was going to have to go around the clock, because I wanted to graduate in two years.

It was very tough going at first, but thanks to my store manager, Mr. Luther Collins, he made my schedule flexible as a frozen food manager to keep the frozen food section full at all times. With that schedule I was permitted to work my own hours.

This schedule was very tough for me, taking college hours each semester, pastoring a church, managing a relatively new marriage, and serving on the Board of Directors of The Tallahassee Urban League. It was only through the grace of God I graduated in the fall of 1972.

A little over two years with a Bachelor of Arts degree and a Minor in corrections. My grades were not pretty, but my determination was. I had help from so many wonderful people who encouraged me including my teacher and advisors, Dr. C. U. Smith, Dr. Victoria Warner, Ms. Nancy Morris, Dr. Jeff Jacks, and Dr. H. D Dillan; the late Dr. B. L. Perry who was President of Florida A&M University; and my wife, Mary, who worked hard for me.

My new church family at Galilee was all helping me in one way or another. I must also give credit to my cousin, Bernice Simmons, who typed all of my papers, the best of which was my book report, about Mahatma Gandhi, the man who defied the Indian government and led thousands of Indians to the Red Sea.

I was an older student with so much going on in my life, and I did not have a college life experience, but I had a real life experience, which my University saw as valuable. So much so that years after I graduated from the School of Arts and Sciences they rewarded me with a spot on their Wall of Distinction. I felt honored to be on the same wall with so many worthy honorees. My preparation for leadership was embedded in my university graduation ceremony in 1972.

In 2009, 27 years after I graduated from Florida A&M University, the University honored me with a Doctor of Humanity and Human Letters, with all rights, honors and privileges hereto appertaining. The honor was bestowed upon me at the same time former President Bill Clinton received his honorary degree. This was an exciting and historical moment for me and my family.

President Bill Clinton, Rev. Ferrell, FAMU President James Ammons

For me to receive an Honorary Doctorate of Humane Letter Degree from my Alma mater Florida A&M University was a great honor. To receive this honor at the same time the 42nd President of the United States of America, President William Jefferson "Bill" Clinton received his Honorary Degree was a double portion of unexpected honor for me. Thank you President Dr. James Ammons and Florida A&M University.

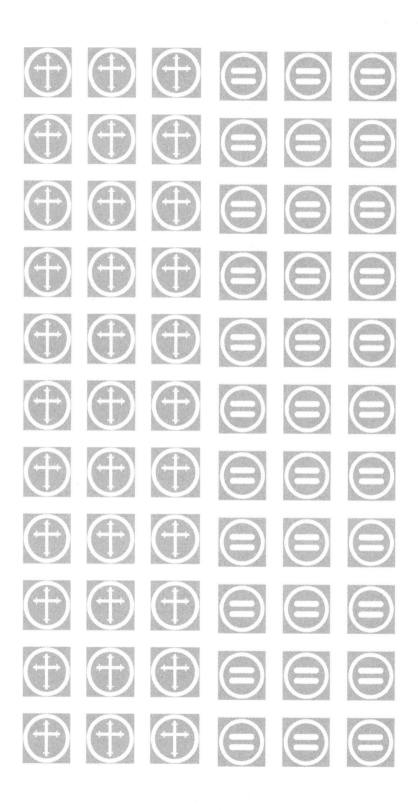

LET THE

EXPERIENCING

OF

LEADERSHIP

BEGIN

Edited by
Mrs. Florida F. Parker

A Challenge in Perry, Florida

In 1971, three years after I returned from serving my country in the United States Army, I was driving my new 1970 El Dorado Cadillac, royal blue with a vinyl half top. The car was one of a kind state of the art. It had a Bose sound system, wood grain dashboard, fully equipped. I am describing this car not because of any vain glory that I needed for what I was blessed to achieve, but because at the time it happened, Perry, Florida, and certain mentalities of the community had a low level of expectations towards blacks and their ability to achieve a higher level of material value. Perry, Florida was known particularly within the black community as one of the more racist towns in Florida. What I was driving would lead to a potentially dangerous situation for a young black man.

With the brief background let me share what happened back in 1971 in Perry, Florida. I was returning from visiting relatives in St. Petersburg, Florida at the age of 35 years old. Little did I know that at the time what model car I was driving and where I was driving could lead me to jail for 10 days or more. Perry, Florida is known for its sulfur wells that give off a foul odor. If you were not aware of the smell, and you had others traveling with you, they would look at you funny.

Once I passed the smell of sulfur, I needed to refill my gas tank. I was headed north to Tallahassee on Highway 27. I spotted a Phillips 66 service station on the left side of the highway where I filled up my tank. As I exit the station from the opposite side I discovered that there was a two-inch embankment about ten feet long where I thought was the proper way out. No cars were coming, no pedestrian was in the pathway, and I could not turn around or back up in the station because another car was coming out behind me the same way. Once I was safely on the other side after driving around the embankment, I had to drive ten feet on the wrong side of the road to get across.

I observed a highway patrolman coming up on the side of the street that I was exiting from. He saw what happened, and I was sure that nothing would come of the situation because I believed that what I did was unavoidable, and I found out later that was a normal occurrence from that station.

What I thought was far from the truth. The officer gave me a ticket for driving on the wrong side of the road. What happened after that will be a story fit for 60 Minutes. Once I received the ticket from the officer, I was furious. When I returned home I sent my fine back with a cashier's check for $26.00. Then I wrote the Governor, my Senator, and Representatives explaining what happened. My biggest mistake was I even sent Judge Grady a copy of the letter. I will always remember it was Judge Grady. In addition to sending him the letter, I also included the $26.00 fine with the letter to make sure that I paid the fine. The judge took exceptions to my letter and converted my fine into a bond and ordered me to come to court for a trial by a six-member jury. The charge was driving on the wrong side of the road.

Now I was becoming really afraid because Perry, Florida was known to be a highly racist, bigoted and hateful city towards black people, especially black men. I consulted with my friend who was a lawyer. He was not able to go with me because he had a prior commitment. He advised me not to worry because the most they could do was charge me the fine that I already paid. He was never so wrong with his advice. Before I left Tallahassee for the trial I made sure I had a thorough physical examination, so that if anything happened to me, my wife would have some evidence that I was abused. My wife was petrified not knowing what to expect and what was going to happen to me in Perry, Florida.

This situation reminded me of a murder trial rather than the traffic violation trial. So I went to Perry, prayed up ready to face whatever the outcome would be. What was about to happen to me would be unthinkable. At best I thought I could at least explain what happened and reasonable people would understand what happened was unavoidable. I realized later, of course, hindsight is 20/20, that only a fool with absolutely no experience as a lawyer should represent himself. The

Judge seated the six-person jury made up of five white women and one black woman. I had charts and diagrams showing the Phillips 66 station explaining what happened. I told the judge and the jury that I entered the Phillips 66 station with good intentions to gas and exit the station from the opposite side from the way I came into the station. I explained in detail. Once I finished no one asked me any questions to cross examine me. The jury was asked to retire and bring back a verdict. This is where it got crazy. Before one juror entered the jury room she turned around and said, "Why are we wasting our time? He is guilty." Jurors went in one door and came out the same door and said, "Your Honor, we find the defendant guilty."

I was devastated. And when the judge announced his sentence I really was afraid. He sentenced me to 10 days in jail to what seemed like a life sentence when I realized that I would be serving that time in a Perry, Florida jail. On my way to booking I had an opportunity to post a bond which would cost me $100 which I did not have. However, thank God for American Express, I did not leave home without it. They accepted the card and I left Perry, Florida and returned home. I used what influence I had with the Governor, who was Rubin Askew, Senator Pat Thomas, the local Sheriff and others. I ended up paying over $1,000 for a $26 ticket and possibly jail time to clear my name and reputation.

What I learned from this situation was never write the judge until your fine has been accepted and the case is officially closed. This experience really was an eye opener for me about the racial challenges that I would face for years to come.

Counseling a Fugitive

In 1971 I was appointed Acting Executive Director of the Tallahassee Urban League, a position that was considered to be very prestigious with high expectation for anyone who serves in that capacity. When appointed to the position the higher profile position caused me to be immediately in the public eye with high expectations from the community.

It was because of that position I received a call from a young white couple who had taken into their home a young black man who was an escaped inmate from the Federal Correctional Institution. The couple was a bit naive and called around to find someone that they could talk to in reference to this young inmate.

They heard that I was a community leader, who was the President and CEO of The Tallahassee Urban League and they wanted to know if I would come and talk with this young man. This family felt that they were helping him and if I would talk to him and hear his concern.

Apparently, he had convinced them that he had been unjustly imprisoned and that he wanted to tell his story. I agreed to come, after all I was a minister, and the newly appointed CEO of the Tallahassee Urban League, the highly respected civil rights organization, what better person I thought to be asked to come.

I, too, was a bit naive. When I arrived at the house of this couple, the wife said that the young man was in the back room of the trailer, which was their bedroom. I did not know what to expect when I opened the door.

I went in, introduced myself and asked him what could I do to help you. He told me how he was imprisoned and he was innocent of the crime. When I first went in, I really did not know at that time that he had escaped from prison.

Once I found out more about who he was, I encouraged him to turn himself in. I would help him as much as I could to tell his story to people I knew who might be able to help him once he got out of prison. I encouraged him that he was still a young man, that he could start afresh and make something positive out of his situation from what he had been through. We had an extensive conversation and at the end he agreed that he was going to turn himself in first thing the next morning. The couple agreed to let him stay there until then. I left feeling like I had done a good and successful thing for this young man. I gave myself high marks on my first encounter with a fugitive on the run. That very liberal couple was also very happy that they were able to help make a difference, hopefully, in the life of this young man. However, little did they know what was to come and how all of these things were going to play out.

On the next morning I received a call from the Tallahassee Police Department requesting that I come down to the Police Department to answer some questions about an escaped fugitive that I talked with last night. They said that the man that I had spoken with had beaten up the couple, left them with multiple injuries needing hospital care The police needed me to identify the man and explain what had happened to them.

What we thought was the right thing to do turned out to be the wrong thing. We were used, the young man really had no intention of doing the right thing. I got a real lesson on preparing for the challenges of leadership and that lesson was to make sure I stay in my lane of experiences and find someone who was trained and had the skills to deal with a situation such as that.

After the dust settled and the young man was apprehended and the young couple was recovering, I continued to do good, but with much more discretion.

The Funeral of an Inmate.

While serving as pastor of the Galilee Primitive Baptist Church in the Chaires community one of my members' brother died. He was an inmate in the Florida Corrections prison system. The family was not financially able to bring the body home, nor attend the burial.

All of this happened in the early part of my ministry at the Galilee Church. My responsibility was not as clear to me as it probably should have been at that time, but I wanted to do what I could to show my support for the family.

In a perfect situation this would not be complicated at all. However, a funeral at a prison without the usual church support, with all of the things that normally happened at our churches during funerals were not available. We all loaded up in two cars and headed to the prison to carry out this service. The delegation included the sister of the deceased, my wife, two Deacons and their wives and a few others made the trip with us. This was a difficult situation, but it had to be done. I had to make sure that I did my best.

In addition to my inexperience as a new pastor, it could not have come at a worse time for me. The day before the funeral I had a minor surgical procedure which caused considerable pain. I should have been on bed rest and no traveling.

The surgery was not complicated, but the pain as a result of the surgery made a very difficult ride to the prison. Even this situation would prove to be minor compared to what we experienced at the funeral.

Once we arrived at the prison and all of the security precautions were completed, we were led to the burial site. The burial site, was truly the most morbid and depressing area of land that I have ever seen. Even though it was a prison, the place they buried this man was like someplace you would throw something out that you never wanted to see again. It was very disgusting. Even a prisoner should not have to have been buried in a location like that. It had a tin plate, like a motor vehicle tag with prison numbers on them, in even rows.

It really looked like death warmed over, was cold, unkept and nowhere would I want to put my worst enemy. Even more sad was the inmates who were the grave diggers who seemingly had never dug a grave nor been given any instructions on how to dig one. The result was basically a hole in the ground long enough and deep enough to dump a body literally in a pine box and it got even worse.

The prison Chaplain who was young and inexperienced, even less than I was, stood by waiting on me to begin the burial ceremony. As strange as it was and as morbid as the surrounding was, it was my responsibility to perform the funeral rites of my member's brother who was being buried. There was no one to say a good or bad word about the inmate, so I said a few words.

I prayed that the soul of my deceased brother will return back to God who created him in his image and likeness. I prayed for strength, for the family to be given reassurance under these circumstances, that God loved them and was there for them to lean on.

Once the prayer was over I committed his body to the ground, earth to earth, ashes to ashes and dust to dust, looking for the resurrection in the last day, and the life of the world to come through Jesus Christ our Lord whose second coming in glorious majesty to judge the world and the earth and sea shall give up their dead and the corruptible bodies of those who sleep in Him shall be changed and made like unto His own glorious body, according to mighty working whereby He is able to subdue all things unto Himself.

Then I gave the benediction, the grace of our Lord and Savior, Jesus Christ, the love of God and the sweet communion of his Holy Ghost, be with you all now and forever, amen.

We all left and never looked back. I will always remember the physical pain and the mental reflection that I experienced for just another preparation for the challenges of leadership for me that were yet to come.

The Dangers of Stalkers

When I became the first black cashier at Winn Dixie Store, the pastor of the Galilee Primitive Baptist Church in 1969 and the President of the Tallahassee Urban League in 1973, my name became a household name; and with that notoriety, came good and evil in people who admired my success and had high expectations for me.

The good you learned to accept with caution because I've learned the hard way that it's only temporary. Those who love you as long as your answers are yes, the love will last. That is temporary love. It can turn to idolizing and stalking and that's where the trouble begins.

I have experienced this kind of love/hate/stalking with many; but for this book, I will only mention four: three women and one man. The **first stalker** was a man who had some serious mental issues, and I was the target of his stalking.

On one occasion, he approached me with some ridiculous conversation. He came by my office, approached the glass door to my office where he could see me behind my desk. So he approached the door and knocked. I tried to direct him to the front area where the receptionist was, but he insisted that he wanted to talk with me, just ask me a few questions. When he insisted, I finally let him in. With a serious look on his face, he asked me: What kind of horse are you riding? Is it a black horse or a white horse? I answered without my pastoral spiritual answer. I said, I'm not riding no damn horse. He laughed and said, "You are riding a black horse." Then he asked me, "Was I going or coming, backwards or forward." I then realized I was dealing with someone I was not qualified to deal with, I did not respond to his last question and he left. From that moment, I knew that it was not the end but the beginning of stalker one. Stalker one started calling me at home and hanging up, and then he would call me late at night and tell me that someone had broken into the Urban League office. When I got there with the police, he would be standing on the other side of the street observing what was going on, knowing all the time that he was the one who had broken the door of the Urban League office.

Once the police put a stop to the breaking in, he chose other harassments towards me. On one particular day after work at the Urban League office, I was working on my personal project, trying to put the finishing touches before the grand opening of the Ferrell's Restaurant which I owned. I was working on a ladder in the ceiling of the restaurant trying to put a light fixture in when suddenly the restaurant door opened and stalker one came bursting through the door straight towards the ladder; and before I could get down, he said to me, "You know I could kill you right now."

I don't today know how I got down Off that ladder, but when I did get down, I headed a few doors down to the restaurant where my brother was working. He followed me step for step, tap for tap until I got to where my brother was. When we came in the door my brother asked me what was going on? I said to him, "Call the police this man is crazy."

My brother asked him what was his problem? He responded, So you call me a MF? My brother said to him, I didn't call you anything. I asked you what's your problem. I called the police. When they got there and cuffed him, he calmed down and started acting rational, and the police took him to jail. Once he got out of jail, the situation started all over again. From time to time, he would appear at the same church where I was attending and stare at me while the services was going on.

On another occasion, I received a phone call from the police department telling me that he was closed up in his house and would not come out without me coming to see him. I would not go, but I did talk with him on the phone and convinced him to come out. And he said he would go with the police if he could wear his minister's robe. The police knew that he had a problem, so they allowed him to wear his robe. They took him to jail again in his black robe. Eventually he stopped bothering me.

Stalker number two, I realize some women have strange fascinations about pastors and other men in positions with substantial influence so they believed. I qualified because I was a pastor, CEO and President of the Urban League, which makes me fit that description. It was out of that context that I found myself caught up with stalker two, one of the first women that begin stalking me. She was a young woman who believed that I belonged to her and that I could solve all of her problems.

It all started when she came to the Tallahassee Urban League seeking help and there was no one on staff available at the time. She requested to see me, with her concerns and I offered my assistance. She needed a place to stay and some emergency food at the time.

Little did I know that helping her would start the whole stalking problem with me because she wanted more than a place to stay and food. Once she was able to secure a place to stay and food, she began stalking me by trying to secure things that she claimed she needed.

One late night she called my house and said she was stranded and someone was trying to hurt her and she needed my help. When I asked where she was, she said she was at a club. I asked my wife go with me to see what was going on.

When we arrived at the location, she was expecting to see me alone; but my wife came with me, and I was glad she did. She asked if I would take her home because she claimed that she was afraid for her life. We took her home and over the next two or three years her stalking became more and more intense.

Calls at work and home continued. Whatever she was going through no matter what it was, she would call me. It took a while for me to separate true needs from true desires. She wanted more from me than just my responses to her calls for help. She had a deep affection for me. After I would not respond to her stalking me, she eventually found other sources to direct her stalking toward.

Stalker number three: From the moment she was helped by The Tallahassee Urban League's staff she asked if there was someone, or did they know of someone they could refer her to for prayer. Automatically staff members recommended me. I had prayed with her and the embracement afterward has led my wife and I down a path or over thirty years of stalking. When she left the office, the stalking was on. First, she returned to the TUL office and asked for me. She wanted my opinion on matters that were not my call to make. I explained that to her, but she was thinking I helped her out of her situation before and she needed my help again. Next she joined the church where I was pastor at that time. She befriended members and my wife and joined the choir while looking for ways to get closer to me. As a member of the choir she gathered as much information about my wife as possible, where she worked, her schedule and the like. She stared calling my wife and other members, being friendly. It was not until one weekend my wife worked that we became aware of her intentions. She came by my house unannounced knowing that my wife was at work. I was unaware she had been to my house, until my neighbor came by later to inform me, that a member of my congregation had been by their house inquiring about why no one answered my door. While at the house she collapsed, and was taken by ambulance to the hospital. I went to the ER. Once I entered her room, the monitors attached to her went off when she saw me. The ER staff immediately asked me to leave.

When she was released from the hospital, the next day she called me, asking for my help in getting her daughter food and her medications. Considering she had just been released from the hospital and not able to take care of herself. I agreed that I would come get those things for her. To my surprise, she opened the door to let me in; she opened her robe, naked. From that very moment I knew that it was time for me to leave and declare no contact at all. Any desire to help her was over.

The stalking continued. She started coming by my house again at night trying to get inside. After trying repeatedly, she gave up, and starting calling my house, writing letters and sending them to the TUL office, stalking the TUL office so much that staff was on alert for her. By now these situations made me realize my challenges for leadership and the stalking that it attracted should not keep me from offering help to those who are in need and pray for those who are in need and request it. What I learned during the course of my experiences with stalker three, was this woman had a bigger problem than I originally thought. From time to time she would stop coming around, and just when we thought she was over her stalking she would become more intense; letters, phone calls, and more unannounced visits at the TUL office.

Whenever she decided she wanted to get close to me, she would always find a way. The longest time she was not around stalking me was when she was convicted of attempted murder. She served a number of years in prison. When I found out about her serving time, it gave me time to reassess the whole situation and wonder was this over. That was farther from the truth than I imagined. While she was incarcerated she did not stop. She sent letters from prison. When she was released she moved with her daughter to another state, and started calling and writing more letters again. She returned to Tallahassee and the stalking began again at the TUL office. She joined my present church while I was away one Sunday. At this point her apparent illness had bloomed. She was in and out of the hospital and mental facilities. This stalker would appear and reappear in church. Deacons and members who were aware of her were on the lookout for her appearance. She has not appeared now for about three years and we are very grateful. As pastor, I love all my members, but in the future, I must be clear that my concerns are for the spiritual needs of their souls no more or less. I pray for stalker three even though she has caused much despair for our church, my wife and me.

Finally, **stalker four** has the same basic story. It all started with my pastoral concern for the people whom I served as pastor, and as CEO. This young woman was a member of our congregation. She had some issues that needed my pastoral counsel. As part of my ministry I am often called upon for prayer and spiritual direction. It was a major part of my responsibility as a pastor to be concerned about my members. A major part of the responsibility of a pastor is to maintain members confidence and respect, because they expect me to preserve their confidentiality.

Many issues are deeply personal and they pour their heart out for prayer and spiritual guidance. Their trust and confidence are placed on the pastor's plate for wisdom and counsel. I have a heart, compassion and concern for the welfare of all of my members. So I would make myself available to listen, to encourage, to pray and provide spiritual guidance. Sometimes when I realize that some of the problems a member might have I am not trained enough to help, I will direct them to where I believe they could receive the right help. I met and prayed with this person and before we finished, like stalker three, again it did not work. Following the meeting I received a key to her apartment with her picture and a note inviting me to the apartment.

I did not respond to any of her letters because I learned from all of the problems before her that any response to her stalking would be interpreted as a positive response to her. My concerns were supported by a friend of my wife's who was a clinical psychologist who counsels students daily in her position at the local University. She said that this person and stalker three could become dangerous and that we needed to be very careful, particularly my wife, because fantasy three had used my wife's name when identifying herself at the mental health clinic. Our friend said that we needed to report this situation to law enforcement in case something came up as a result of what has been happening with me and my family.

Stalker four helped me appreciate the special people who cared for and treated mental challenged people. It also helped me to realize that God works in mysterious ways. When he exposed me to these unstable people, he did it to help me prepare for the challenges of leadership which would expose me to people who were not always on the up and up in life.

Their motive, at best, is to make sure that your life is miserable and whatever they can do to make that happen, knowingly or unknowingly, they will do it.

MY

FIRST

VISIONARY

EXPERIENCE

WITH

GOD!

Called to Preach

My first visionary experience. Back in the late 1950s, I was fascinated with dramatized radio stories and Randy's gospel stations where they played gospel music late every Sunday night. I would never miss Randy's, especially the gospel hour. The highlight of Sunday night was just before the station would go off the air was to play one half of *The Eagle Stirreth Her Nest*, by the late Reverend C. L. Franklin.

The first half of the sermon would be a story. Just as the sermon was getting good, you would have to wait until the next Sunday to hear the other half. Once Reverend Franklin got things stirred up, Randy would remind the audience to tune in next Sunday night for the conclusion. Gospel singing and gospel preaching, especially Reverend Franklin, were always a highlight in my life. I loved quartet singing because I had a group called the Walls of Zion. We were called to sing all over Tallahassee, Georgia, and other places.

I was the lead singer along with my brother, James, my cousin, Wesley, Augustus Johnson, and Charles Thompson. We were well-known. In the beginning we did not have music or musical instruments. Most of our singing was done a cappella, and we would keep the beat by patting the sides of our bodies. This was why it was so important for me not to miss Randy every Sunday night to hear the latest in gospel music and be prepared to rehearse some of those songs with my quartet group.

Reverend C. L. Franklin preached *The Eagle Stirreth Her Nest* each Sunday night. On this particular Sunday night I remember very well just after the second half of Reverend Franklin's sermon, I fell into a deep vision and in the vision, I saw an image like a large ball of fire headed straight towards me. I did not have time to duck or get out of its way. However, I did not have to because the fiery ball came through the closed window of the house and stopped directly in front of my face. A clear voice out of the ball of fire spoke to me and said, "I want you to preach my gospel like C. L. Franklin preaches, with power, clarity, conviction." Without hesitation, I said "yes Lord I will preach the gospel of Jesus Christ" and the rest is history.

Pastoral Leadership

Pastoral leadership requires that a real pastor must be called and commissioned by God to prepare him to be full of the Holy Ghost, equipped to teach and serve. He needs to have genuine faith. Joel like qualities, Solomon like wisdom and knowledge. He must be full of the Holy Ghost.

He may not have ever had formal training in psychology or ophthalmology, but he is often called upon to handle issues of the mind or see invisible sights. He may not have a medical degree, but he is often called upon to respond to issues that affect the hearts of his congregation. A truly committed pastor understands his calling and he responds with the power of the Almighty God who created him in his image and likeness.

The pastor who loves God and the people that God gave him to serve demonstrate each and every day his calling through his love and his compassion for his people. A good pastor and a good preacher are not always the same.

For example, a good pastor electrifies his members with the power of the spoken word, and he also shows his members by example what the word of God can do when it is followed. A good preacher is not always a good pastor because he may not always have the best care for his people in his heart, for his heart may be in the emotion from electrifying responses from the word.

There is much more to pastoral leadership than preaching alone. Preaching, teaching and following is what makes faith work. Pastoral leadership was the beginning of my challenge for leadership. I used all of the preparation for the challenges of leadership that I experienced from my brother spraying me trying to kill a fly, encounter with a vacation in Miami, first black cashier and all of the other events leading up to where I am with this book.

I have learned so much over the last 44 years of my pastoral experience, even though I have not had formal training in many of the areas that I am called upon to respond to. Through prayer and the assurance from my Lord and Savior Jesus Christ, he always comes through for me.

The Lord will never allow me to become caught up in my own success with the members I serve, because self-serving as so many do, the Lord reminds me that it is not about me, but rather it is about the source of where we get the power from and that source is through Jesus Christ.

Over the course of my life whenever I became uplifted in myself rather than the Lord, he reminds me that my calling is from the Lord and not from me.

To make sure I get this message, he reminds me. One morning when I went to the bathroom to brush my teeth, I discovered that I had a return visit from Bell's Palsy, a stroke like symptom that caused my mouth to pull my face to the right side. I asked the Lord to remove it, but he said no, he could not remove it.

He removed 95 percent but it was a reminder that He was in charge of my life and that if ever I got what my mother used to call the big head, Bell's Palsy would remind me that God is in charge. A pastor's work is never done. He is on the clock 24/7, and no excuse is accepted by his members.

Those who are faithful and those who are not, the membership expects the pastor to be available whenever called. It does not matter what time day or night, they are expecting you to show up when they call. A family member is sick, a family member dies, some member is in trouble, marriage problems, financial problems, death in the family, these are just a few of the many issues that face a real pastor every day.

Pastoral leadership for a successful church is not always measured by the number of members or ministries, but rather successful pastoral leadership is determined by the level of stewardship of its members, where souls are saved and the kingdom of heaven is added to. Then and only then is our pastoral leadership successful.

First Church Pastored

My first church in 1969, after I returned from serving in the United States Army as a soldier and as a minister, I had maintained my spiritual identity while in the military. I reunited with the church and I was able to get back to preaching in my home church, Testerina Primitive Baptist Church.

My pastor, the late Elder G. W. Hill received me back with open arms. One Sunday morning during devotion at the Testerina Church, the pastor and I were in the study getting ready to go into the sanctuary, when a tall, mixed grey headed man asked the pastor if he could speak with me briefly for a moment.

Pastor Hill recognized who he was and said it was okay to speak with me. That man was Deacon George Proctor, Sr., from the Galilee Primitive Baptist Church in Chaires, Florida. Deacon Proctor said to me that the Galilee Primitive Baptist Church was without a pastor, and the church went in prayer and the Lord led their hearts to ask me to consider serving as the pastor of their church.

I was not prepared to accept such a direct spiritual calling from a church that I had never heard of before, did not know where the church was or any history on the church. The Lord overshadowed me and before I knew anything about the church or its people, I said if the Lord says so I would be willing to serve.

I said to the deacon I have no experience as a pastor, but with the help of God and from my church I would be willing to work with the Galilee Primitive Baptist Church if I am called to be its pastor.

The process for selecting a pastor was more than the chairman of the Deacon Board contacting me. The following procedure had to be followed. Other candidates would be considered, and given a hearing. The association had a candidate it wanted to consider, but the people wanted me. They went through the motions and the procedures, but when the process ended I was the church's overwhelming choice to become their pastor.

I was ordained by the Old West Florida District Association and I began my first pastoral responsibilities in 1969. My challenges of leadership began.

The very first Sunday that I begin leading the congregation at the Galilee Primitive Baptist Church, a small rural community located in Chaires, Florida, about eight miles from Tallahassee, I could feel the excitement in the air and the love in the people toward me. I was very tense, so I asked the deacons where was the bathroom?

To my surprise he said the bathroom was out back to the left of the church and the bathroom was an outhouse. This would probably be difficult for many who read this book to understand, but an outhouse is a toilet without running water and no plumbing.

This was common in rural locations. I made my way to it through the tall grass. Suddenly I did not have to go anymore. It was that very moment my first challenge of leadership began.

Once the service was over I called the deacons together and said to them an outhouse is not acceptable and whatever it takes next Sunday we will have a bathroom inside the church. My pastoral leadership started rolling. And with the help of God and the fellowship of the people who worked together by the next Sunday we had inside bathroom facilities.

Remember the unexpected with the rat situation, the outdoor out house was one of those moments where the unexpected happened again with me. What happened with the toilet was the beginning of many challenges here at my first church. After the first year at Galilee, our congregation began to grow in size and in influence.

I remember the very first revival we had and my first candidate for baptism. The challenge that I faced was the location the deacons were using. I was used to baptizing in a big lake not far from my membership church, Testerina. I was in for a big surprise.

Galilee was baptizing underneath a bridge down from the church. When we arrived at the bridge I asked the deacon, was this location safe? His answer was not reassuring because he said as far as he knew it was safe. At the time I had to suffer it to be so.

The service began with devotion. While devotion was going on I was scanning the bridge and I saw a few beer cans floating by along with some trash. Once devotion was over the deacon would walk out into the water and put a stake in the ground where the baptism would take place, where it was safe, and the water was deep enough and safe for the preacher and the candidates.

I had much trust in the Lord, but very little trust under the bridge. We got through it all right, but once again I called my deacons together and said we will not baptize ever again under a bridge. All of our next baptisms were held on a private lake owned by a Christian woman who gave the church permission to use it as long as we wanted to without any charge.

My next challenge for the Galilee Church came when I made a proposal to build a new fellowship hall. The Chairman of the Deacon Board suggested that I consider instead of building a fellowship hall, building a new church and use the existing church as a fellowship hall. That was an excellent idea that I supported and the church supported as well. This would be a major challenge in my leadership.

Galilee was a very small church with very few people, but our faith in the Lord was very strong and the work began. First we needed a plan. The Lord worked the plan out in an unusual way. He used the benefit from my internship while serving as pastor I was also doing my internship at the Federal Correctional Institute, a Federal prison in Tallahassee. I was a student at Florida A&M University.

During the course of my internship I met a young white male inmate who was serving time for a blue collar crime that he had committed. I did not know what he had done, but we became friends. During the course of my time with him I discovered that he was an architect. When I told him about what we were doing at the church and we needed a set of plans. He agreed to draw the plans for us.

I described what I wanted the church to look like. I wanted the church ceiling to be lit up in the form of a cross that would run the length of the church, with the wings covering the deacons' side and the mothers of the church side. This was something never before done in a church. I was not sure the prison system would allow the plans to be drawn, but the plans were drawn using the prison materials and supplies. The plans were completed and I carried them out of the prison with the Institution blessing, we begin building the new church sanctuary.

The second challenge that we faced before the church was completed was the foundation. We were blessed to have had the Chairman of the Deacon Board, Deacon George Proctor, who was an employee of the railroad company. He had a great relationship with the railroad company and was able to secure discarded rail road tires for the foundation. Deacon Proctor knew how to dig out the foundation, and with his skills and a friend in the community they worked together and set up the foundation using railroad ties to secure the foundation and the flooring. From the foundation to the complete block work, most of the labor and work was done by volunteers from the church and the community. We worked together day and night.

The next building challenge came when a major storm resulted in a flood, water descended upon the church. It was almost impossible to get within 50 feet of the church. I was determined to get to the church because the work had to be done and I kept working.

In the evening after school and after internship, I drove as close to the church as I could and waded the water to the church. The water from the flood came within one inch of reaching the partial board flooring in the church. One inch higher water and all of the flooring would have been destroyed.

The next challenge came while I was working on the pathway from the old church to the new church. I was nailing down the flooring and not thinking about anything but completing the work while under flooding conditions. The spirit of the Lord said to me, look up, and when I looked up a moccasin snake was looking down at me. I remember crying out, I believe, oh Lord, but I don't know if you can hold me to that statement. Whatever I said must have been in snake language because the snake went one way in a hurry and I went another way in a bigger hurry.

With determination of the people who had a mind to work and the guidelines from the Almighty God we completed the church on time and within the resources that we had available. These are just a few of the many challenges I faced at Galilee Primitive Baptist Church.

To tell all of the challenges from this experience would require a book all by itself, but for now we gave all the glory and honor of this church building to God, our Savior, Jesus Christ, who directed our path to the success we had during the years that I was blessed to serve this congregation. To God be the glory for the things he has done.

"My Second Visionary Experience with God"

THE VISION BEGAN WITH THIS

Kleman Plaza Fountain, Tallahassee

THE VISION FULFILLED WITH THIS

MY
SECOND
VISIONARY
EXPERIENCE
WITH
GOD!

Second Visionary Experience

And the Spirit of the Lord came to me as I passed Kleman Plaza in downtown Tallahassee, Florida. The vision focused my attention on a round, mushroom shaped fountain. The water from the fountain was overflowing completely over the edge of the fountain with an even sheet of water, almost like the screen from a movie theater or a television. The Spirit showed me moving pictures on the face of the water. I was moved by what I saw as those pictures seemed to transform those images into spiritual functions that would glorify God in the most profound way outside the church ministry walls.

When I saw the fountain, I envisioned Moses and the Burning Bush, that is when I realized what the vision was saying to me. Many people who might not ever come into the traditional church for worship pass the church late at night when the doors are closed, and the minister and other church leaders are not available. Those who pass by can visit the visionary fountain. This fountain will be available to help fill the void for many who need counseling, prayer, and other inspirational motivation when they have nowhere to turn.

The vision was clear to me. I needed to find a way to transform this vision into an instrument of service to the one who made the vision possible. The question to me was, "Where would I start to make this vision a reality?"

The questions to which answers were needed, "Is it possible to project moving images on running water?" and "How would those images be able to produce sound coming from the water?" I was confident that it would be a matter of time before those questions would be answered, because the Lord gave me that vision and it is my calling to make it work.

The very first thing I did was contact Robert Charles, a graduate from Florida A&M University School of Architecture, who now owns his own business. I provided him with a preliminary sketch of what I thought would work. Robert scaled the drawing, and converted it to an architectural graph. He also researched the possibilities of projecting pictures on a moving waterfall. His research found an expert who had developed many water-screens for fountains in major building projects and lakes, but never something quite as we envisioned.

The water screen expert was Charles Garrity. His expertise was the major link in developing the vision. The original design was modified to fit the location of the fountain, and the development process began! From the day I first saw the vision until the night the project was completed and the first picture was projected on the water, my heart burst with joy.

I prayed and gave God the glory for the fulfillment of His vision and that He used me to show the world that all things are possible when we trust God. Many people will benefit from this revolutionary ministry that will help the downtrodden, the homeless, the ones who have lost their way, and the poor in spirit to find some comfort by just pushing a button outside when the church doors are closed. Please come and share this vision with me and all who share the Kingdom Building Mission and those who love the Lord.

The Second Church Pastored

In 1992, I was called to pastor the Saint Mary Primitive Baptist Church. The experience that I gained from the 23 years at Galilee Primitive Baptist Church was much different, but in many ways the same. At Galilee I had few major challenges because there were less than 100 members to work with. We worked through those challenges with very little difficulties, and we had great cooperation.

However, at St. Mary Church I had more members which meant that I had more to deal with. More counseling, more weddings, more funerals, more family crisis, and more operational challenges. Pastoring at St. Mary Primitive Baptist Church made my trust in God stronger.

Pastoral leadership to a larger congregation and with people who sometimes feel they can serve in a pastoral position better than the pastor can, and when that happens I have to remind the church that my calling to this church was not my doing, but rather it was the Lord, Jesus Christ and that is my duty to lead and not to follow. And when I fail in my official capacity to lead, God will find another place for me to exercise my gift and talents.

Leadership in a church is different than leadership in a professional business. In business success is measured by how much profit you can generate and how happy you can keep your stockholders. Pastoral success is measured by how many people you had a spiritual impact on, how many stewards were developed from your ministry. What affect your teaching had on the people who listened to your teaching. How many people were baptized who truly repent their sins and had their faith in God deliver them.

All of these things matter along with the fact that a pastor has to really say no when many want to hear him say yes. He has a biblical measuring tool that he goes by and that tool is the Bible. When you have to stand firm on what is right based on the word of God, it sometimes has a tendency to make your value and your stock go down, and that love members expressed initially sometimes reverses itself.

Those who love you at first sometimes take a different attitude at the end. Those who didn't like you at first also have a tendency to reverse and become people that respect you more than they ever did before.

When you are a pastor you take the bitter with the sweet, the good with the bad, and the success with the failures. My leadership challenge with St. Mary Primitive Baptist Church began with excitement and support. The installation program was of the highest quality, unique in its presentation, different enough to be noticed and noticeable enough to be different.

I wanted to please God and impress the members that I would be leading for years to come. So far so good. Leadership at St. Mary provided me a wealth of spiritual growth and appreciation from the preparation of leadership I learned as recorded in chapters before this. Pastoral leadership can sometimes be overwhelming because of the individual differences in the families and church environment where I served.

For individuals and families in the city for the most part the value system is different. Strange as it seems, the rural church members seem to have a stronger faith in God based on their experiences, whereas the church in the city seems to have less faith and they should be the ones I think, should have the most faith because they have had more positive experiences as it relates to their environment than perhaps those who are in the rural areas. Yet I notice a complete difference between the two areas of pastoral leadership.

This theory seems to hold true even as it relates to gospel singing that I have done for years. Gospel singers in areas of the country that had more depression and more issues facing them, racial and otherwise, seem to be more determined and more gospel focused than those persons who have had less experiences and less trauma in their lives.

The gospel singers in Mississippi, Alabama, and Georgia seem to be stronger in their convictions about what the Lord had meant to them and what the Lord has done for them. The singers from other parts of the country were different. Their worship and praise was different, not as exciting and not as determined, yet it was faith that was real and genuine but their determination seemed to be less exciting than the churches in Mississippi, Alabama and Georgia were experiencing.

This by no means meant that either location, their salvation was not secure in their faith in God, just a difference in how they expressed their faith in God. The challenge of leadership at St. Mary Primitive Baptist Church began with very minor situations to me, but very uplifting to some of the congregation members.

When I began my leadership responsibilities I did not want to undermine anything that the former pastor had done. He served for over 33 years before I was called, I was recommended by him so I served with caring, made no immediate changes in leadership of the church. I respected what Elder Richard Matthews leadership had accomplished.

There were a few things that I could not live with. So I changed two things almost immediately when I became pastor. First, there was a big painting of a picture of Jesus directly behind the baptismal pool that I removed. The second thing was a piano that was placed into the walls of the choir stand, and the pianist's back was turned to the choir. I took the piano out of the wall and placed it on the floor of the church. These two issues were overwhelmingly supported by the membership. However, there were a few who did not support the idea. The removal of the piano got the most attention from the musician who said that she would not continue to serve as musician of the church unless the piano was returned back to its original position. This became a very sensitive issue with those few people who had issues making it even bigger than it probably was.

I learned from my previous experiences that any issue no matter how small it seemed to appear to others, must be resolved quickly before it festers and grows into something much bigger than it should.

So I recommended to the church that their faithful musician for the many years that she had served be given a plaque and expression of thanks for her services. The piano was placed on the floor of the church in a position which complemented the choir and the congregation, the picture of Jesus vanished.

The next major challenge came when the Lord showed me a vision of a building and a fountain that would be erected in front of the church as an outside ministry for the large number of people who would probably never come into the church, on any given Sunday. See the faith fountain in the book.

The vision came in the early part of my pastoral leadership at St. Mary. When I expressed my vision to the church congregation, most of the membership again were very supportive and excited about the vision. I was willing to pay as much as I needed to pay because I believed that the vision was divinely given to me, and I was confident that the Lord would see it successfully completed.

To cut down on some of the concerns from those who were not willing to support the vision they would not be asked to help bare the cost as long as they did not encourage others not to support the fountain. The fountain was completed.

Since I was installed at St. Mary in 1992, well over 1,000 members have joined, hundreds baptized and some moved on to other ministries and other churches. Many are still faithful here at Saint Mary. It is a fascinating journey that I have been blessed to serve. I found spiritual growth and development every time I counsel a family, during their moment of grief because they had lost a son or a daughter, a family member who is addicted to drugs or caught in a crime.

I am touched when I officiate a wedding or visit a hospital and provide comfort to a family whose loved one is terminally ill and hope of recovery is in the hands of the one who created him/her. I am elated during our morning worship when our children come down for prayer. When I question them and listen to some of their answers then I pray especially for them that God would bless them, protect them, guide them and lead them in a world that is not always friendly to children.

I am even more touched when a family brings their children to be blessed and give their lives back to God who gave them life. Pastoral leadership is more to me than what is sometimes seen by others as just a good sermon calculated by the time it takes to deliver and how much money he receives from such a short time on Sunday.

A good sermon is a great thing, but pastoral leadership is more far reaching than the Sunday morning message that is received. It has a lot more to do with what happens during the week, what happens during the time between the Sunday morning sermons? There are so many other variables in a real pastor's responsibilities that cannot be calculated in dollars and cents.

Real pastoral leadership is often lost in the shuffle from teaching and preaching and living so that others can see your good works and give glory to God for our stewardship. So that others can see the light and accept the Lord, Jesus Christ as Savior.

When we lead others to Jesus Christ we are fulfilling Joel's prophecy. "That I will pour out my spirit upon all flesh; and your sons and your daughters shall prophesy, your old men shall dream dreams, your young men shall see visions," Joel 2:28 part B.

When the Lord prepared me for leadership He gave me what I needed to lead His people where He wanted me to take them. Without Him, I would have failed many times over, but his words are true. When he said, "Teaching them to observe all things whatsoever I have commanded you: and, lo, I am with you always, even unto the end of the world. Amen." Matthew, 28:20

What is a Primitive Baptist?

Before I talk about all of the many challenges that I faced as President of the Florida State Primitive Baptist Convention, I want to answer a basic question that many of my friends and others have asked over the years. Just what is a Primitive Baptist?

My first position with the National Primitive Baptist Convention before I was elected President, I was Chairman of the Arrangement Committee, and the committee on this particular year chose to broaden the convention outlook by expanding the locations of the convention.

We had an opportunity to go to Buffalo, New York. In our planning we made an effort to involve other churches and other church denominations in our convention by sending a special luncheon invitation to pastors in the Buffalo area. All invited pastors were from other denominations. We had a number of pastors who attended.

Once the luncheon began one of the pastors could not hold his question any longer. He said I have heard a lot about Primitive Baptist, but tell me, just what is a Primitive Baptist? I responded, a Primitive Baptist is AME, a Missionary Baptist, a Church of God in Christ, a Presbyterian, a non-denomination, even Catholic and all Christian churches.

We all have two basic things in common. In each of these denominations some of the members are going to heaven and some are going to hell. The other thing that we have in common is that we all share a common belief, we believe that Jesus Christ is the son of God, He was born from the Virgin Mary, He was baptized by John the Baptist. He lived, he died and on the third day he rose from the dead and declared that all power in heaven and earth is in his hands.

We all stand firm with our faith and our belief that that is true. Denomination is a preference, determined by many factors, including family background, where we worship, our environment, where our parents went to church. I chose Missionary Baptist where my father worshiped. When he died I joined my mother's church, which was Testerina Primitive Baptist Church. At the time I was only ten years old.

So denominational preference did not mean very much to me. I just wanted to be where my mother was. As I grew older denominational preference became more important to me and the Primitive Baptist denomination was where I was comfortable and satisfied.

Primitive Baptist doctrine means original, first, which fits right in with the gospel of John, Chapter 1, verse one, two and three. In the beginning was the word and the word was with God and the word was God. The same was in the beginning with God. All things that were made were made by Him and without Him was not anything made that was made.

That is original. That is first and that is Primitive Baptist. Primitive Baptist churches have been around close to 200 years. The National Primitive Baptist is over 100 years old. So we are not new people. We are not Primitive Baptists because we are not smart. We are Primitive Baptist because we have been smart longer. We are not about our denomination, we pray for all believers that one day when the Lord returns we will all be prepared and ready to meet Him.

The Primitive Baptist doctrine includes three ordinances. They are Holy baptism, Holy communion, and Holy washing of the Saint's feet. Most denominations exclude washing of the Saint's feet. Some sparingly, because all denominational preferences believe in the things that Jesus practiced, but did not practice washing the Saint's feet. We believe that what was good enough for Jesus, is good enough for all Primitive Baptists and others.

Primitive Baptists have 16 articles of faith. We believe, one, that there is only one true and living God and the trinity of persons in the God Head, Father, Son and the Holy Ghost, and yet there are not three but one. God

Article Two, we believe that the scriptures of the old and new testament are the Word of God and the only rules of faith and practice.

Article Three, we believe in the doctrine of eternal and particular election of a definite number of human race and chose in Christ, who chose Christ before the foundation of the world that they should

should be holy without blame before Him in love.

Article Four, we believe in a covenant of redemption between God the Father and God the Son.

Article Five, we believe in the fall of man and the communications of Adam's sinful nature to his posterity. Ordinary generations and their impotence to recover themselves from the fallen state their are in, by nature, by their own free will and ability.

Article Six, we believe that all chosen in Christ shall hear the voice of the Son of God, and be effectually called, regenerated, and born again.

Article Seven, we believe that sinners thus born again are justified in the sight of God alone by the righteousness of Jesus Christ imputed to them by faith

Article Eight, We Believe that faith is the gift of God, and good works the fruit of faith, which justify us in the sight of men and angels as evidence of our gracious state.

Article Nine, we believe that all the saints of God justified by the righteousness of Christ shall preserve in grace, and none of them finally fall away so as to be lost.

Article Ten, we believe in the general judgment both of the just and the unjust, and that joys of the righteous shall be eternal and the punishment of the wicked shall be everlasting.

Article Eleven, we believe that the visible church of Christ is a congregation of baptized believers in Christ adhering to a special covenant, which recognizes Christ as their only lawgiver and ruler, and His word their excusive guide in all religious matters....

Article Twelve, we believe that the spiritual officers of the church are the pastor and deacons whose qualifications and duties are defined in the epistles.

Article Thirteen, we believe that baptism is the immersion of a believer in water by a proper administrator in the name of the Father, Son and the Holy Ghost.

Article Fourteen, We believe that only an ordained Elder has a right to administer the ordinances of the Gospel, such as have been properly baptized, called, and come under the imposition of the presbytery by the authority of the Church of Christ.

Article Fifteen, we believe that only regularly baptized and orderly Church Members have a right to communion at the Lord's Table. Article Sixteen, we believe in washing of the Saint's feet in a church immediately after the Lord's Supper. All 16 of the articles are supported by the word of God.

So you ask, what is a Primitive Baptist? These are the things that we value the most as Primitive Baptists. We are not ashamed of our faith and we hold true to it.

Elevation Through the Ranks of the Florida State Primitive Baptist Convention

From preparing for the challenges of leadership, to experience the challenges of leadership is by far the most trying and hardest experiences that I have dealt with so far in this book.

Leadership in the place you would expect or think would be the least stressful was by far the most discouraging and draining that I have ever experienced. Even though it was the most challenging, it was also the most rewarding. It really taught me how to lean heavily on the Lord and invoke his powers to sustain me and send me through and get me through with success and spiritual growth and development.

The Florida State Primitive Baptist Convention and the National Primitive Baptist Convention started me on my experiences as a leader in the top operations of our denomination.

My very first position came after the Florida State Convention Secretary, my good friend, Elder Jeremiah Gee died. Elder Daymon was the Assistant Secretary left the Convention and started his own ministry which left the door open for me to be appointed an assistance secretary and shortly thereafter elected as the secretary.

I remember my secretarial skills were not that good, but my ability to get help and much prayer and overnight review of my minutes, by the next day I had covered all of the flaws and no one really knew how bad my minutes were. I became more and more efficient as the years passed by until my name floated around as one of the upcoming young preachers in the Convention.

I was a college graduate, pastor of a small but recognizable church, I was a gifted preacher who was not afraid to speak up on issues that I had concerns about. When my predecessor's leadership became stagnated and the Convention was at a standstill, the visionary leadership had lost its vision and new leadership was needed to rekindle the fire that had dwindled down to ashes and needed to be re-stirred.

Of course, that did not go well with our President who was serving his 33rd year. When the Vice-President who had served with the President for years moved back to his home in Texas, the Vice-President position was vacant and my name came up for his replacement. Against the President's support I was elected Vice-President where I served for five years under the President, who did not want me on his ticket, but the Convention voted me in anyway.

You can imagine what that was like for me and the Convention. I served under him with great admiration for what he had accomplished and where he had led the Convention over the years.

After serving under the President for four years and the President's strong arm of leadership became less than effective, the people wanted a change. I made it known that I was interested in becoming the next President of the Convention.

I became even more interested when a situation involving another Elder of the Convention who ran into some problems and the question was asked of the president, what should we do with this brother, should we forgive him? The president had no compassion for the brother and so when he messed up and it was his time for reconsideration, the convention remembered how he handled the previous situation and it led to him being voted out and I was voted in as the next President of the Convention.

And that is where my experiences in leadership with the Florida State Convention began. At least two Elders of the Convention were not happy with my election as president and they were willing to do everything they could to short circuit my leadership.

It started an assault on my character and ability to serve. They sent me a long letter critical of moving the convention to the hotels. What they did not know at the time was what they were doing and saying only made me more determined. I used all of my Urban League experiences and training to lay out the convention based on the National Urban League format which had a long history of proven success. The Urban League was several times larger than the Florida State Primitive Baptist Convention. So I was able to build upon something that was already successful and use that as a model to provide the Florida State Primitive Baptist Convention the benefit of my experiences.

The first convention was held in a hotel in St. Petersburg, Florida. We began with an eloquent reception called the President's Reception, different from punch and cookies we have had over the years. We had shrimp, roast beef, food trays, vegetable trays, and cheese trays. All of the servers were walking around providing people with food as they entertained themselves, no alcohol, of course.

We had a beautiful ice sculpture with the three R's which represented our theme. Rekindle, restore and renew, the gift that is within us for Kingdom building. The event was out of the park so to speak. We were able to attract major sponsors.

One particularly was Winn-Dixie. The first convention set standards high for years to come and emulate. Attendance was up, the finances were up, spiritual satisfaction was on the rise. People were excited about this convention perhaps more than ever before.

From the beginning to the end the first convention that I presided over was an exciting, great convention, in addition to the largest number in attendance, financial increases. The new program format we started with pre-convention workshops included building healthy church schools with Mavis C. Cook Publishing Company. Building church structure with the late Dr. David Henderson, evangelism and outreach with Elder Kenneth Duke.

The workshop was well-attended with the welcome and exciting acceptance from the convention. With such a strong showing at my first convention I knew that our convention had to always top the first convention, which set the standards for years to come.

With much prayer and hard work we wanted to always plan our convention with the vision and sanctioned by God. So from the theme to the program content I always consulted God for direction and guidance.

Year two of my State Convention presidency, which was the 94th session, the theme was, "It Is Time to Use the Salt, Shine the Light,

Be a City On a Hill for Kingdom Building." This resonated from Matthew 5:13-14. The message was, the 94th annual session of the Florida State Primitive Baptist Convention last year, we all rejoice in the glory of the Lord as he gave us the most successful convention ever in spirit, in finance and in fellowship.

Thank you, Jesus. I want to thank all of you for your cooperation and support of our new administration. Last year's successes are history fully recorded in the minutes of the 93rd annual session. The 94th annual session is before us and we must move forward with deliberate speed.

The theme for the 94 session was, "It Is Time to Use the Salt, Shine the Light and Be a City on a Hill for Kingdom Building," Matthew 5:13-14. This theme is a powerful mandate to the Christian community in Florida particularly, and the rest of the world to change the world for the better.

I am confident that when we work together we can change a large number of the community problems which includes crime, drugs, diseases, violence and other things that are deteriorating our society. For us to move forward with such blessed assurance that Jesus is ours and that he has provided us with the tools necessary to change the world for the better. God bless you and have a great convention.

The 95th session theme was God's amazing grace is sufficient for Kingdom building. The message was recorded earlier. The 96th session, theme was "Mount Up with Wings as Eagles for Kingdom Building." The message was recorded earlier.

The 97th session under my leadership was, "Go Ye Therefore and Teach All Nations For Kingdom Building." The message was pre-recorded earlier.

The 98th session theme was "Work While It Is Day, When Night Cometh No Man Can Work For Kingdom Building." The message was pre-recorded.

The 99th session theme "Mustard Seed Faith Can Move Mountains for Kingdom Building," The message was pre-recorded.

The 100 Centennial session theme, "100 Years of Kingdom Building." The message was pre-recorded.

The 101st session theme "Lord, Make Us One As You Are One" The message was pre-recorded.

All of the convention themes, from the 93rd session all the way through to the 101st session, principle focus was Kingdom Building. For all that we do is for the building up of the Kingdom of God where we all want to enter one day.

Each theme was carefully selected based on the needs of the time, on the circumstances with which the convention was confronted and based on God's revelation to me to make sure that those themes were used properly and given out at the proper time.

The convention grew stronger each year and those who were disappointed at the success of the convention, they grew as well. I had to be subjected to so many underhanded, self-serving innuendos and false accusations and blatant untruths from those who are in my cabinet and a strong force within the layman department. I got very little support from my very own association and the state, the statewide leadership was trying to unseat me as well.

The undercurrent had really gotten bad just before I was seeking my last term as President. The word had gotten out that a key position in my administration the Chairman of the Miracle Hill Nursing and Convalescent Home would be removed.

The person was also the second Vice-President of the Convention in my cabinet. To short circuit my position the nursing home leadership conspired with the second Vice-President and they sent out a 25-page report strongly implying that I had misused the convention funds for my own personal use. The report had no collaborating evidence. Even though the report was proven to be untrue, the damage from the report resulted in me loosing the election.

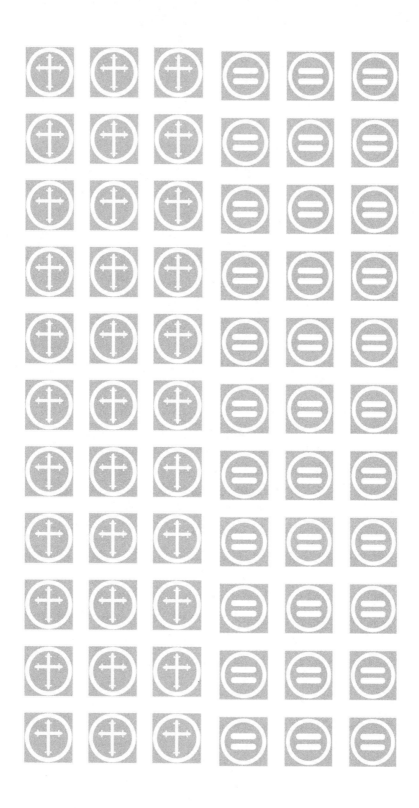

NINE YEARS

OF

PROGRESSIVE

LEADERSHIP

Florida State Primitive Baptist
Convention Sessions Begin

The experiences that I received with all of the issues leading up to experiencing church issues there were none comparable to the close encounter, with the rat, the spray gun used by my brother to spray the flies, the trip in New York, picking beans, the funeral that was held at the prison, nor any of the other experiences that I had compared with the experience of dealing with the hierarchy of the Primitive Baptist Church, were all in a class by itself.

The place that I would expect my experiences to be the less or the least confrontational ended up being the worst. When I was elected President of the Florida State Primitive Baptist Convention following the State President who had served for over 33 years, this experience in itself was more than met the eyes. My new cabinet, my new leadership team began under severe scrutiny from those who were upset about the results of my presidential election.

Those few who were in opposition to my presidency raised all kind of issues, trying to dethrone me before I even got started. My challenges to lead the Florida State Primitive Baptist Convention started in 1993, at our annual session held in St. Petersburg, Florida, followed by the sessions in 1994 in Jacksonville, 1995 in Pensacola, 1996 in Miami, 1997 in Clearwater, 1998 in Panama City, 1999 was in Ft. Lauderdale, and the 100th Anniversary in Jacksonville, Florida, where the Centennial Celebration was held.

The final year of my presidency ended in Daytona Beach where I was voted out by those who were willing to go to any extent to make sure I was no longer in leadership. It worked temporarily. They did it for evil. One year later I was elected President of the National Primitive Baptist Convention.

The 93rd Annual Session of the Florida State Primitive Baptist Convention

Recap my Florida State Primitive Baptist Convention leadership as President. It all began in St. Petersburg, Florida. The theme was, Rekindle the Fire, Restore the Joy, Renew the Right Spirit In Me for Kingdom Building, taken from Psalms 51: 10-12.

Following the leadership of my predecessor who was the Convention visionary for over 33 years and provided outstanding leadership. I recognized his contributions and my intentions were to build upon what was there rather than to tear down what was there.

The changes that I made were not made just for change sake, but rather to improve the leadership and build upon what my predecessor had left. Without a doubt the Founding Fathers of this great convention did not need a new leader who would tear down the foundation, but who would build on the existing foundation.

My challenges were to use what was in place and begin my first year as its leader with encouragement and motivation by rekindling the fire, restoring the joy and renewing the right spirit within all of us for the right reason which is Kingdom building.

My prayers were that we should began the convention, with some new programs, move vigorously, strongly implementing God's Holy Words, and providing the people on the mountains of despair, new hope for a better life, a better nation and a better world.

I invoke the reminder that through God's word we have the power to positively impact those who are victims and perpetrators of crime and drugs that are destroying our neighborhoods, our state and the nation. The new agenda included a new program from the beginning through the end.

The attendance was up by 30 percent, the finances up by 25 percent, and spiritual motivation up by 100 percent. With but a few detractors, the very first convention under my administration was a success.

The 94th Annual Session of the
Florida State Primitive Baptist Convention

To use the salt
Shine the light
Be a city on a hill
For kingdom building
MATT: 5:13-14

Florida State Primitve
Baptist Convention
94th Session

My experience with the challenge of leadership proved to be even more challenging than the 93rd session. When expectations are high, everyone expects the same positive results.

When the Florida State football team won its 29th game in a row, the expectation was that they would win again. They never expected to lose the 30th game; of course, they did. My administration was somewhat in the same position in 1994.

We were very successful in the 93rd session, and the people were looking for something better in the 94th session. We did not disappoint them. We met the challenges head on and the results of the 94th session were even better than the 93rd session. I challenge the convention to move forward with deliberate speed to live up to the new theme. It is time "To Use the Salt, Shine the Light, be a City on the Hill for Kingdom Building", from the scriptures, Matthew, 5:13-14.

Last year's session is now history and we must move forward with the blessed assurance that Jesus is ours, and that he has provided us with the tools necessary to change the world for the better. The session was a powerful mandate to the Christian community, particularly in Florida where we all serve our churches, but our influence can change the world.

The 95ᵗʰ Annual Session of the
Florida State Primitive Baptist Convention

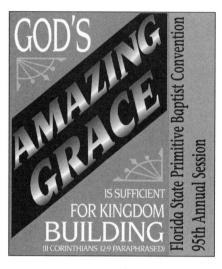

The 95th session theme was, "God's Amazing Grace is Sufficient for Kingdom Building. II Corinthians, 12:9, paraphrased." The 95th session was confronted with issues related to two ongoing problems the Primitive Baptist Camp, our camp and the nursing home owned by the convention. These two issues alone required a delegate approach to resolution.

If we worked with all involved to assure that these two projects would continue to be used. I encouraged the cooperation from each association, pastor and all of our churches affiliated with the Florida State Convention. The camp result was restored and nursing home was expanding. The Amazing Grace of God completely revealed itself and the experiences that I gained was priceless. To God I gave the glory.

When hostile people used everything they had to try and stop the progress of God's people, they were not successful. I did not think it could get any better than what I was experiencing with the Florida State Primitive Baptist Convention. My strong faith in God has continued to evolve. The more experience I got from these situations the stronger my faith in God continued to evolve, and the amazing results from what God can do to enhance the growth and development of the Florida State Convention.

The 96ᵗʰ Annual Session of the
Florida State Primitive Baptist Convention

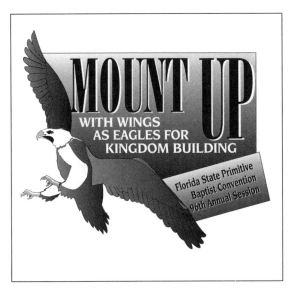

The theme of the 96ᵗʰ session of the Florida State Primitive Baptist Convention was, "Mount Up with Wings as Eagles for Kingdom Building." I encouraged the delegates, pastors and convention supporters to work and pray and exercise their faith in the Lord. I believe that positive results are predictable and assured by the words of God that teaches us that all things are possible with God.

My goals for the 96th session were to work together for a much closer fellowship with each other, allow the influence of the Holy Spirit to rain down on the convention, encourage the attendance of over 1,500 to each service to increase the financial support by 30 percent. All of my recommendations were reached and some exceeded expectations, and the experiences of leadership continue.

The 97th Annual Session of the Florida State Primitive Baptist Convention

The theme for the 97th annual session was, "Go Ye Therefore and Teach All Nations in Kingdom Building." For the theme I challenged each Convention leader to move the Convention to the next level of service and commitment.

We needed to unify our strength, resources and spiritual power, to raise enough funds to begin planning for a State Convention headquarters and Convention Center. I was convinced that with the number of churches, church members and human resources and influence working together the plan to build could be achieved.

I was asked by senior pastor, is this project your vision or God's? I responded to him, I believe that God is directing me. I am convinced that what we are planning to do is His will. With six years of successful leadership I believe my experiences and the challenge of leadership let me recognize that everyone is not on board with the plans.

I encourage those who could see the vision to move forward, and those who could not see the vision not to tear down or hinder those who were willing to move forward.

The 98th Annual Session of the Florida State Primitive Baptist Convention

The theme for the 97 annual session was, "Work While It Is Day, When Night Cometh No Man Can Work For Kingdom Building. John 9:4."

The 98th session continued with my encouraging each local Primitive Baptist delegation, pastor, layman, Women's Congress and convention supporters, that we must work while it is day. When night cometh no man can work. I ask all convention supporters to unify over the next three years to build the convention headquarters, hotel and restaurant within the next five years.

With God's power I am convinced that there is nothing too big for God, when we apply our faith and our works while it is day. There is nothing impossible with God on our side. Everything that we need God has it. The funds, God got it, the materials, the plan, the builders and the work needed. I assured the convention that we could make our plans work when we work while it is day.

The 99ᵗʰ Annual Session of the Florida State Primitive Baptist Convention

The theme was "Mustard Seed Faith Can Move Mountains for Kingdom Building," Matthew 17:20 paraphrased. We experienced an unusual moment in history, a millennium year which we have never seen before and never will see again. We are blessed beyond hundreds and thousands.

With this new hope and a renewed spirit that God will lead us to higher heights and deeper depth, with mustard seed faith we look forward to seeing mountains of descent move away, mountains of doubts moved away, mountains of despair moved away. I look forward to seeing mountains of hope coming forward, mountains of joy coming forward, mountains of peace coming forward, mountains of forgiveness coming forward, and the Seed of Faith reaching its peak for Kingdom Building.

Mountains, mountains, get out of Florida's Primitive Baptists' way because we are coming and we are coming with power, enthusiasm and perseverance.

The Centennial Celebration
of Kingdom Building

The Centennial Celebration marks the highest point in my experience in the challenges of leadership. It will take all of what the Lord had taught me to get through this 100th celebration.

Eight years under my leadership required ultimate planning and implementation of the plan for the Florida State Primitive Baptist Convention Centennial Celebration. It will also determine if I learned enough to carry out such an awesome responsibility that will lead the convention to its full potential.

This event was held in Jacksonville, Florida. Each of the six associations was identified with a designated flag and color. Each of the flags was carried by a designated leader of each Association. A 100 voice choir was established for the celebration. The National Primitive Baptist Convention President, Dr. T. W. Samuels, was the guest keynote speaker.

This Centennial Celebration was the highest level of experienced leadership that had ever been demonstrated in the history of the Florida State Primitive Baptist Convention. My administrative leadership paid off.

The successes we had up until the Centennial Celebration only fumed those who were in opposition, and the very next year they were successful in their plan and plot to make sure that I was not elected for the next presidential tenure.

The 101st Annual Session of the
Florida State Primitive Baptist Convention

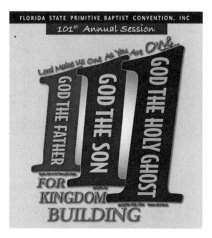

The theme for the 101st Annual Session of the Florida State Primitive Baptist Convention was "Lord, Make Us One As You Are One." It was the year of the disaster for our nation in New York, Pennsylvania and Washington, D.C. With much prayer, fellowship and the love of God, we survived those attacks.

Last year's Centennial Celebration carried us to an exciting spiritual confirmation that God continues to answer our prayers. Surely He was with us and His anointing power impacted the convention from the beginning to the end. The display of unity among its pastors, churches, associations, and members were all breathtaking to watch and be a part of.

I encouraged the convention to pray that God will make this year's theme, Lord, Make Us One As You Are One, a reality in our fellowship, praise and worship services. We must not fail in our efforts to become one people for different functions, but for one vision. I called upon the members of my cabinet, the Laymen Congress, Women's Congress, Youth Congress, Church School Congress, Ushers Congress and all to embrace the challenge of oneness throughout the convention.

It was at the 101st Session held in Daytona Beach, Florida, that my tenure as president ended. I was eligible to serve one more year as President, but those who believed that I was a threat to their position of power would be lost if I served another three year term and they were right.

My experience for the challenge of leadership fell short and the vision was deterred by God with His blessing.

NATIONAL PRIMITIVE BAPTIST CONVENTION, USA, INCORPORATED

Edited by
Mrs. Margaret M. Jones

A firm hand at the helm

The new president of the National Primitive Baptist Convention will keep his faith rooted in tradition

By Radhiya Teagle
DEMOCRAT WRITER

As national and local churches splinter over homosexuality and doctrinal issues, the Rev. Ernest Ferrell, the new president of the National Primitive Baptist Convention, says that "the vision is clear" for the direction of his church.

Ferrell, pastor of St. Mary Primitive Baptist Church on Georgia Street, campaigned on the themes of accountability, respectability, leadership and building character within the Primitive Baptist Convention, or, in his words, "kingdom building." The convention has 1,600 churches and 500,000 members throughout the nation. Ferrell's outlook won him a unanimous vote for the presidential chair of the convention, and he is described as a "visionary" by his peers.

When asked if he foresees his church splintering over homosexuality or other doctrinal issues, he said, "No, not in my lifetime."

And when asked if there were any gays in leadership within his church he said, "I suspect there probably are, but I stand on this: Either you believe the word of God

MIKE EWEN /Democrat files
The Rev. Ernest Ferrell leads St. Mary Primitive Baptist Church in Tallahassee and, now, his denomination's national convention.

or you don't. You can't pick and choose."

Ferrell, 61, has served as pastor of St. Mary Primitive Baptist Church for the past 13 years. Before that, he served for 23 years at Galilee Church in Chaires. He also served a 10-year period as president of the Florida Primitive Baptist Convention USA, succeeding the late Elder Moses G. Miles of Tallahassee, who served as president of the state convention for 30 years.

While his leadership style may seem firm, Ferrell is described as a leader who puts others at ease.

"Ferrell is a person that understands leadership and relaxes the reins on others," said the Rev. Robert Crocker of the Hills Tabernacle Church in Nashville,

Tenn., who is also assistant secretary of the Primitive Baptist Convention. "He knows how to let people do their part and make their own decisions. He's not trying to do it all himself."

One issue that is important to Ferrell is what he perceives as a change in attitude toward the church and church leaders. That's something he wants to address within the Primitive Baptist Church.

Ferrell, 61, says he remembers a time when people sought the church for answers, but now he feels that the church is looking outside its walls for guidance. "Our guidance and direction must come from God. The authority as pas-

Please see FERRELL, 2D

"Our guidance and direction must come from God. The authority as pastors and leaders of the church seems to be diminishing, and we must do everything we can to change that."

— The Rev. Ernest Ferrell

122

The National Primitive Baptist Convention, USA, Incorporated President Elected

When the dust settled from the Florida State Primitive Baptist Convention, and I had gotten over the betrayal of members of my cabinet and others who plotted to get me out of the presidency of the convention, it was time to move on.

When President T. W. Samuels announced that he was not running again for president of the convention because he was retiring, I made it known that I would be seeking to be the 11th president following Dr. Samuels. The tradition served me right, after serving nine years as vice-president under Dr. Samuels that I should be able to win the election. I did not take the fact that I was vice-president for granted considering what had happened in Florida. Tradition does not always repeat itself, especially as it relates to me and the circumstances that I had endured.

My track record with the convention while serving as vice-president, I believe gave me the edge. I chaired the Executive Board and provided oversight for the Arrangement Committee when we broke new grounds for planning the convention. I broadened the convention locations, got major concessions from hotels, built in special benefits from hotels and the local business bureau, got support from major partners, including well-known sponsors as Winn-Dixie, attorney Willie E. Gary, Citizens Bank, and the former Mayor of Birmingham, Alabama, Richard Arrington, Jr.

We received economic incentives from hotels even though many were not in support of the impact the Arrangement Committee had those who were reaping the benefits were not complaining. I was running against two other candidates who believed they would win as I did. Experience as vice president and CEO of the Tallahassee Urban League and vice president of the convention for nine years gave me an edge of what I could use to my advantage.

My platform was about what the Lord gave me from the Florida State Convention, the church where I pastored and currently pastor, was Kingdom building, accountability, respectability and leadership. My central focus was the vision is clear. With two other candidates in the race I won with 51 percent of the votes, no run-offs were necessary.

The challenges of leadership continued to develop and the detractors continued to mobilize against me. I continued to be determined to press on towards the mark of the high calling. My experiences never stopped coming and, my praise to God for all that he had done for me never stopped.

My first challenge as new elected president of the National Primitive Baptist Convention was to develop a national program worthy of the Lord's approval and with support from the majority of the convention leaders. My visionary plans were number one, to raise our spiritual stock in Kingdom building for Jesus Christ our Lord and Savior to a higher level; number two, to educate our children and ourselves through our faith and the founding fathers' vision that set high standards in Christian education, evangelism and church growth; and number three, to clearly understand that our faith is embedded in the Word of God. Our 16 Articles of Faith have stood the test of time. Our three Ordinances of Faith on which we stand are Holy Baptism, Holy Communion and Holy Feet Washing Rites. All three of these were examples that Jesus Christ gave to us to follow.

Jesus was baptized by John the Baptist. He had communion with his twelve disciples in the upper room, and after the communion had ended He took a towel and girded Himself and began to wash the disciples' feet. If it was good enough for Jesus we believe it is good enough for us to do. Jesus said if you know these things blessed are you if you do them.

The convention administration started with the same vigor, the same spirit, and the same level of support it did when I was elected president of the Florida State Primitive Baptist Convention. Each year from the time that the Lord gave me the leadership position, we always had a strong theme and each one of the themes were prayed about, blessed by God, and put into practice.

The 99ᵗʰ Session of The National Primitive Baptist Convention, USA, Incorporated

The theme for my very first session as the 11th President of the National Primitive Baptist Convention began with the theme, "Building up the Kingdom of God, tearing down the strongholds of Satan", Exodus 34:13-14.

The theme's mission for the National Primitive Baptist Convention was prayerfully chosen because I recognized that Satan has a stronghold on the nation and the world and I wanted Satan to know that his stronghold was coming down because the word of God has the power and the will of the people to tear down what Satan has acquired and replaced those strongholds with the truth, and the truth will set you free.

The theme also launches my long standing vision of Kingdom building, accountability, respectability and leadership, and it is now my time to implement the vision that I have had for years from the State of Florida.

The vision is clearly and succinctly defined by our Lord and Savior, Jesus Christ, that we as followers of the Word of God must focus our Christian attention on working to build up the Kingdom of God and tear down the strongholds of Satan. The Lord on many occasions instructed his man of God to tear down altars and cut down strongholds of Satan, particularly in Exodus 34:13-14, but ye shall destroy their altars, break their images, and cut down their groves for you shall not worship any other god, for the Lord, whose name is Jealous, is a jealous God.

In the New Testament Jesus told his disciples in Matthew 28:18 and 20, all power is given unto Me in heaven and in earth. Go ye therefore, and teach all nations, baptizing them in the name of the Father and of the Son and of the Holy Ghost and teach them to observe all things whatsoever I have commanded you, because I am with you always even to the end of the world. Our responsibility to the Kingdom of God is to work vigorously each day to tear down the strongholds of Satan.

My challenge to each of us is to begin now with determination to succeed in this missionary way. We can do it. I am convinced that my selection as president of the National Primitive Baptist Convention was not by accident, My responsibility as a leader was to implement the mission and the vision God gave me, I know that with the help of God and, the your support, of the people of this great Convention, we can move mountains of despair, and mountains of trouble. We can invoke the power of the One who made us in his image and likeness. I challenge every one of you pastors, teachers, supporters, the nation, and the world to move forward in bringing down the strongholds of Satan. We are working to destroy all of the little pockets of evil that are now present in our world, in our state and in our nation.

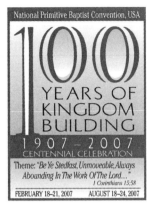

The 100th Session of The National Primitive Baptist Convention, USA, Incorporated

The Centennial Theme

The National Primitive Baptist Convention began with my talk with the Lord for the challenges that the convention experienced over 100 years; the trials, the tribulations, the pitfalls, and the forces of evil which did not want the Primitive Baptist churches to rise above ground, above its name Primitive Baptist.

However, it is certainly true that the Lord's word teaches that nothing is impossible with the Lord on our side when we are steadfast, unmoveable, always abounding in the works of the Lord. As I Corinthians 15:58 says. In the words of Maya Angelo, "yet we rise." With this prayer the Centennial Celebration began and a Centennial capsule was placed in isolation for the next 15 years.

The Centennial Prayer

Dear Lord, we come before you as humble as we know how, thanking you for life, health, strength, and a clear mind which lets us realize who we are and to whom we belong. We thank you for the joys that we have experienced in serving you, God. We thank you for our ups and our downs, our successes and our failures. We thank you, Lord, for the good and the bad days of our lives. We are encouraged by our positives and negatives because we know that whatever we experience in this life is all about our Christian growth and development and our closer walk with you, Lord.

Lord, we are grateful that you have spared our lives to see and experience this 100 Year Celebration, which is a milestone in our lifetime. Your grace and your mercy have kept us, shaped us, and molded us into what you would have us to be. We give all the glory, honor and praise to you, and you alone because you are truly worthy to be praised.

We thank you for the sacrifices you made for us when you gave your only begotten son, Jesus Christ, our Savior and our Redeemer who suffered, bled and died that we might have eternal life. He is alive and lives in our hearts, and because He lives our forefathers' prayers are answered. Because He lives our hopes and dreams of that day when all of God's people will unite on that "great getting up morning," the realization of your word will ring true. "And God shall wipe away all tears from their eyes and there shall be no more death or sorrow nor crying, neither shall there be anymore pain for the former things are passed away." Revelation 21:4. We thank you, we praise you, and we love you. To God be the glory! Amen.

From that prayer, the Centennial Celebration began with singing, worshipping, peaching, teaching, and fellowshipping with our brothers and sisters from across the Nation. May God bless the National Primitive Baptist Convention of the United States of America.

The 101ˢᵗ Session of
The National Primitive Baptist
Convention, USA, Incorporated

The theme was ,"The Greatest Gift of all is Love, I Corintians 13:13." The 101ˢᵗ Session of the National Primitive Baptist Convention continued moving forward toward my long vision of Kingdom Building: Accountability, Respectability and Leadership. The growth of the 101ˢᵗ Session was on a steady course of progress. Attendance was up, finances were up, and the presence of the Lord was in the sessions. The membership of the convention was breaking records in attendance. The greatest gift of God was ever present and the anointing of the Holy Ghost was fresh upon us each day of the convention. Of course whenever progress is being made, there is always someone waiting to find a way to short circuit any recognizable progress. Conflict only needs just a little confusion and the rest is opportunity. The 101st Session kept the evil forces at bay and the Words of God took care of the rest, who dared to challenge God. The Lord blessed the 101st Session from the beginning of the convention to the end. We demonstrated our love for the convention, our love for each other, and most of all our love for God.

The 102nd Annual Session of The National Primitive Baptist Convention, USA, Incorporated

The 102nd Session of the National Primitive Baptist Convention continued my uphill challenges and experiences in leadership. The development of the convention always presented new challenges each year.

When you think you have everything where you want it, new conflicts are always waiting in hibernation for little conflicts to emerge. The 102nd session was no different. However, my determination only grew stronger. With every given challenge and experience the Lord always prepared me for the challenge.

The 102nd theme was, "Wait on the Lord: Be of Good Courage and He Shall Strengthen Thine Heart," Psalms, 27:14 . The words of God teach us that waiting while you are working is the central focus of our convention theme. Wait on the Lord, be of good courage and he shall strengthen thy heart.

While we are waiting on the Lord He is renewing our strength because of the challenges ahead of us. The challenges of a multimillion dollar convention headquarters, a ministers leadership conference, a women conference, a youth conference, the building of new churches and missions in major locations where we presently do not have churches were the main initiatives of my administration. I stressed the importance of increasing income support from state conventions and associations are all important in meeting the critical challenges we will face.

All of these challenges can be accomplished by utilizing funds from the convention church expansion and auxiliary development funds. I know that waiting on the Lord will increase our strength, especially when we are working while we are waiting. Waiting without working is none productive. Working while waiting is progress.

"Therefore, my greatest challenge to you was the right to raise our hands with the strength from faith in God and see what the Lord will do for the missions set before us. For I am convinced that with a little faith and much work we will rejoice from the victories ahead of us.

There is no need for the convention to be timid in our dreams because we are working for the greatest power source available. We are in the Army of the Lord. There is no greater power, no greater resources, no greater knowledge than that of the only true and living God who created us in His image and His likeness. So how can we fail when we trust God?"

The 103ʳᵈ Annual Session of The National Primitive Baptist Convention, USA, Incorporated

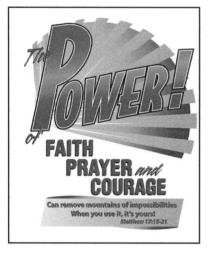

The theme for the 103ʳᵈ Annual Session of the National Primitive Baptist Convention was The Power of Faith, Prayer and Courage, "can remove mountains of impossibilities when you use it…" Matthew 17: 15-21. This theme reassured the Christian community that the balance of power is in the hands of God, and the use of His power is available to those who have faith in Him.

It also demonstrates daily to a misguided world It cannot change the inevitable destiny of God's purpose and His plans for those who believe and for those who do not believe. God demonstrates His power every day when we experienced a volcano eruption in Eastern Europe which brought flames down out of the sky; the earthquake in Haiti that turned buildings into rubble; and the oil spill in the Gulf of Mexico that unleashed just a sample of his oil upon the shores of Louisiana, Alabama, and Florida to name a few examples.

God's power turned off the volcano ashes when He decided. He stopped the earth from shaking in Haiti when He wanted. He provided the engineers a blueprint to design the right cap to stop the oil spill in the Gulf of Mexico. These displays of God's power are only opportunities for the Christian community to demonstrate its faith in the powers that God gives us to move mountains of impossibilities.

We cannot stop the volcanoes in life, but our faith can plug up the holes. We cannot stop the oil spills from reaching our shores, but our faith and work can surely clean them up. With our united faith, prayers and courage we have the power when we use it. If a little faith can move mountains, what are the possibilities when we have much faith?

My brothers and sisters let us use our God given powers to make our world a better place, and our people a better people. This theme is our answer to the problems we are facing as a nation, as a state, as a community, and as a family.

Each day we are growing closer and closer to the conditions that were faced by the children of Israel. The conditions they faced and even in the story of Cain and Able could not be imagined as to what our world would look like today. It is time for the people of God to rise up and rediscover the sources of power the Lord has given us, and if we use them for the building of the Kingdom of God here on earth we can stand back and see the glory of God rising up as it has done many, many times before. To God be the glory.

The 104th Session of The National Primitive Baptist Convention, USA, Incorporated

To confirm my tenure as president of the National Primitive Baptist Convention our themes were God given and Holy Ghost sanctioned.

The theme for the 104th Session was "Praises to God for His Greatness Power, Glory, and His Victory and Majesty." My tenure as president ended in the 104th session of the National Primitive Baptist Convention, six years of experiencing the challenges of leadership with the convention.

The Lord reaffirmed that my leadership, and the impact He allowed me to have on a convention that had drifted somewhat into a routine operation and a vision that had somewhat dimmed. God gave me new marching orders when I assumed the leadership of the convention.

First, he invoked my God given vision of kingdom building accountability, respectability and leadership. This had been a reoccurring vision for my six years as president of the Florida State Convention. I was blessed and successful to implement the vision for over 12 years.

Now that my tenure was over as President, my leadership and experience with the convention continues with the St. Mary Primitive Baptist Church where I am serving my 23rd year as pastor.

My message to the 104th Session of the Convention was, "we are blessed and thankful that the Lord has included you and me among the living and highly favored so that we may experience another moment of life. I thank Him for all of us. I pray that once this convention is over, we will all return to our locations of the country and use what we have learned, the compassion, the forgiveness, and the understanding with Christ and exemplify that everywhere we go, and God will bless us abundantly." Thank you.

We must follow His example of love, compassion, forgiveness and trust. If we fail in any one of these examples our convention will suffer. I am confident that we will meet all of our challenges and we will, by the grace of God, be successful in resolving them all.

God bless all of you is my prayer.

When Loyalty Doesn't Mean Much

When I was elected president of the National Primitive Baptist Convention in 2002, it was one year after I was voted out as president of the Florida State Primitive Baptist Convention. I was excited about serving and I had the opportunity and privilege to pick someone that I believed would serve with me, and was an upcoming pastor who pastored one of the largest congregations in our convention.

If I had known what I know now, I would not have chosen him as my running mate. When I recommended him the convention accepted my recommendation and he was voted as vice-president of the National Primitive Baptist Convention, USA. I really did not discover much about my choice until many years later, as it became more and more apparent that my choice was not the right choice. He was my choice at the time, but time proved that I was not really his choice.

The role of a vice president is a very prestigious role. First, the vice-president serves as the chairman of the Executive Board of the convention which serves during the interim of the National Convention General Session. He serves as the chairman of the Arrangement Committee. Each of these positions is very prestigious in the Primitive Baptist Convention.

As chairman of the Board of Directors he is responsible for providing leadership to the convention during the interim or during the period in which the general convention is not in session. Therefore, this position is paramount to actually being next in charge or in some cases, in charge of the general convention.

He is also responsible for the oversight of the Arrangement Committee and plans the convention site for the coming year. I began to take notice of my vice president because he never really took charge of his responsibility of oversight of the Arrangement

Committee and never responded to the convention planner. He never really took responsibility for the leadership position at all.

The more I learned about my vice-president, my partner, the more I realized that he really was not in my corner. When the opportunity for him to respond to the issues we were facing, he never really came to my rescue, but I overlooked it and thought it was just a matter of immaturity. But as time moved forward I realized that he was planning all the time to take what I had for himself. I was a bit naive to think that all of this was just a matter of immaturity, but of course that proved to not be the case.

I would always look out for him. I provided a special spot on the convention agenda. He was given Friday night at the Close Out Session exclusively for him, but he did the unthinkable. He decided that he could not wait until his turn to be elected president. He decided to run against me when he knew all the time that I was eligible for another term. In the one hundred year history of the National Primitive Baptist Convention the vice-president had never run against the president. He always waited his turn, and was in a position of support. He decided to run without consulting with me, nor did he resign his vice-president position while he was a candidate for the presidency.

I tried to make myself believe that what was happening would be short lived and the convention would see through the vice-president's actions. Little did I know that the vice-president and others who had been a part of his campaign had conspired to pull together one other candidate to run with him. This candidate had not been successful for two elections to be elected president and they had, I believe, gotten together, knowing that if they ran together they would split the votes and would be able to win.

The amazing thing about that whole process was the person who ran with the vice-president for the presidency had run for president two times before this time, and knowing that he was not going to win, but said the Lord told him to run. When you have a successive defeat by a large number of votes, then your motive has to be for other reasons, and those other reasons allowed the vice-president to become elected president by only seven votes.

When I asked the person who ran with the vice-president against me why did he run when he had lost twice before, he said that the Lord told him to run. And I asked him if the Lord told him to run; He then knew that you were going to lose. Of course, the person got pretty upset and made some strange responses to my question. His responses to my question made me sure that it was a conspiracy between he and the vice-president, because he became very indignant and said to me that he supported me, which he did not when I was president.

When I lost the election I was devastated, more from the disloyalty from the man I had carried with me as my vice-president for six years. This was the second time this happened to me. First, with the Florida State Convention and now with the National Primitive Baptist Convention, especially when the convention was at its highest point of notoriety, spiritual connections, financial connections, and attendance. The three major issues that helped determine the success of the convention were at their highest peak, and our convention was admired by other conventions and denominations.

This reaffirmed my position that all of this happened based on jealousy and envy. It took a while for me to accept what happened, and my human instincts wanted me to respond in a verbal way, but my spiritual insight gave me a Godly response and reminded me the same God who made me made them as well, and the Bible says that we must pray for those who despitefully misuse you, and with this in mind I eventually was able to pray for all of those involved.

My prayer was that the Lord would give them a repentant spirit and that they would apologize to the convention to me for what they did, and how they split the convention. As I prayed that prayer, my life was vindicated and I was determined to move on. I also prayed that the Lord would touch the hearts of the general convention members so they would recognize that what was done was not acceptable and that the convention would rise above envy and jealousy and move on with a better program for the convention and for our Lord and Savior, Jesus Christ.

How to Get Over Betrayal

The election outcome really floored me because the person that I had trusted to be my running mate decided to run against me, knowing that I was eligible to run for my final three years according to the time limits. After three years the vice president would run with very little opposition. This would follow the tradition of 100 years.

The action by the vice president was a classic example of what betrayal really was like for the convention and me. This action by the vice president was unethical, non-Christian, and it did not reflect the character of a preacher who preached with power, clarity, and understanding. To do this against his brother who had trusted him for over six years as his vice-president, and even further when I was president of the state convention, he was the Bible Expositor for the State of Florida.

A man of God who knows better but did not do better. I must admit betrayal really does hurt. The person who gave him the opportunity to serve under my leadership, was not easy to swallow. I tried to understand how he thought it was important for him to run against me and not wait for his turn.

I always treated him with respect and I believe that he should have received honor when honor was due. I loved him as a brother and as a man of God. The more I tried to justify his action, the more I was hurt. It took me several months to accept the actions of betrayal by my vice president. What really helped me to get over my feelings of betrayal was when I realized that my experience was second, third, fourth, fifth or twentieth place or more when it comes to the betrayal that Jesus Christ had when Judas, who was a part of his cabinet and was a part of his inter-circle, betrayed him.

Judas served as treasurer for the band of apostles. As His disciple he was given power against unclean spirits, to cast them out, to heal all manner of sickness and all manner of diseases, and Judas questioned Jesus about the ointment that was used by Mary to anoint Jesus' feet, and wiped them with her hair. He said that the ointment could have been used or sold and given to the poor.

Jesus recognized Judas would betray him when he said one of you is a devil. Throughout my six years serving the National Primitive Baptist Convention, I should have recognized that my vice president was not loyal to me, nor was he appreciative of my leadership, and all of the time he was prodding to be president himself.

Once I realized what Jesus went through and He was and is the Son of God, surely I have no right to be surprised at what persons will do when they are envious and jealous. They will do anything to get where they want to be and to put their names in leadership positions.

It was after much prayer and seeking the guidance of the Lord, I began to pray that the Lord would lead my vice president and others to repentance and cleanse my heart from any ill-will against him and others who participated in his scheme. I also had to pray for the convention that seemed to have accepted this disloyalty and betrayal with business as usual.

Betrayal must not be allowed to destroy my ability to forgive and move forward, because without forgiveness it will only make your life miserable when the unforgiving person goes on with their life as usual. If you want peace of mind always forgive. Leave the retribution in the hands of the Lord.

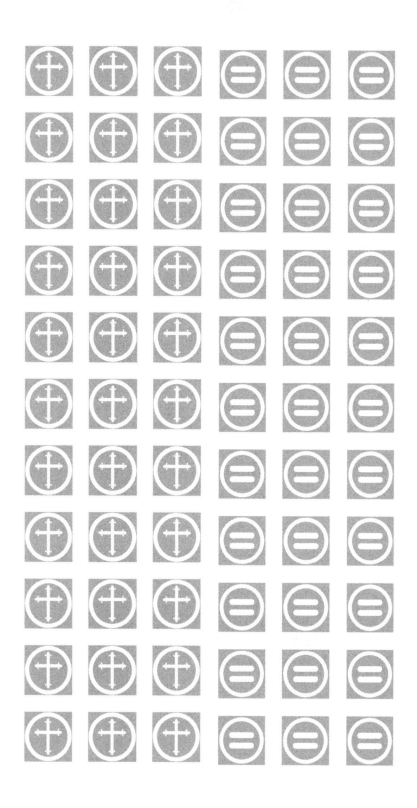

MY
NATIONAL
URBAN
LEAGUE
EXPERIENCES
IN THE
MOVEMENT

Appointment to the
Tallahassee Urban League
Board of Directors

In 1970, two years after I graduated from Florida A&M University and two years after serving in the United States Army, I returned to Tallahassee and was asked by Dr. B. L. Perry, Jr., President of the Florida A&M University, at the time, to serve on the Tallahassee Urban League Board of Directors.

I did not know anything about what the Tallahassee Urban League Board of Directors was or what the Tallahassee Urban League was about. The fact that the President of Florida A&M University asked me to serve on the Urban League Board of Directors, I felt honored and I agreed to consider his request.

I tried to figure out why I was asked to serve. I had no prior knowledge about the Urban League. So the only reason I could think of was the notoriety that I received from being the first black cashier and recently called to pastor a small church.

I agreed to serve. When I came on the board, I came with a very good friend of mine, the Reverend Leroy R. Thompson, a local pastor who was very well-respected in the community. Reverend Thompson was the pastor of the Gethsemane Missionary Baptist Church where all of the college students were worshiping.

Both of us attended our first meeting of the board members with representatives from a cross section of the community, mostly PhD's, attorneys, professional business owners, Reverend Thompson and I. After observing the level of professional and well-credentialed people on the board, I was trying to see how we would fit in.

It did not take long before I became entrenched in the urban league and dedicated to what the urban league was all about. This was new territory for me, but I became completely dedicated to making a difference with the urban league movement. It became my all as it relates to community involvement.

Dr. Perry observed my excitement and the hard work I did as a volunteer. He decided to step down as president and no one else would accept the position. So he recommended me as the new president of The Tallahassee Urban League. That is what it was called at that time, and the rest of my beginning with the Urban League is now history. My commitment has continued to be in the best interest of the movement and the best interest of those the Urban League serves.

Rev Ernest Ferrell prays for President George W. Bush

A Prayer for President George W. Bush

I prayed for the President of the United States of America, George W. Bush when called upon by the National Urban League Conference leadership who called on me for prayer in numerous situations. After the first two years of my attendance at the National Urban League Conference, under Vernon E. Jordan's tenure, he asked me to open the convention with prayer at our annual family session. The family session is where all of the board chairs, presidents and CEO's, building members, and thousands of volunteers assemble together for family session. The family session was spiritually motivating.

The late Betty Stubbs would sing and play gospel songs and music. Sometimes we would have a local choir. It was the emotions and togetherness representing Urban Leagues from across the country. It was my responsibility to read a scripture and pray the family prayer.

Sometimes a local pastor would be asked to come in and bring the message. The family session was the pacesetter of the week for the convention. At the first family session I was asked by Vernon E. Jordan, to pray for the family session which continued through President John E. Jacob, President and CEO Hugh Price, and our current President, Marc Morial. They all seemed to have favored me from the beginning. Probably because I was only one of two ministers that were also CEO's.

I like to think they saw in me a person of strong faith and presented myself always in a respectful way. My prayer for the conference was that the Lord would bless the conference from the beginning to ending, that God would bless the convention leadership, those CEO's who work everyday in the trenches trying to make a difference in the lives of those who were not always in a position to make a difference for themselves.

One of the most memorable experiences I had with the National Urban League Conference was during a planning session of the conference. I would from time to time be asked to provide the invocation at the Quarterly Century Club Meeting and other meetings. In one particular session, President George W. Bush was going to speak. We were all waiting for the session to start. At that time President Bush was not very popular, but the National Urban League understood the importance of diversity because whoever is occupying the White House needed to know who we were, and what we stood for as an agency. We always treated whoever was in leadership with respect, whether we differed from them or not.

While we were waiting on the president to arrive a group of CEO's and NUL staff members came towards me and asked me to come with them. I did not know what was going on. My heart was racing. I thought that something had happened to my family. They marched me to the speaker's waiting area where program participants were all gathered to go in and on the stage. Then I saw President George W. Bush, and Mark Morial asked me to come over and meet the President. And he asked me if I would bring the invocation and pray for the President before he spoke.

He asked the President if he minded if I would pray for him. The President said, "no, he didn't mind, because the President needs prayer as well as everyone else."

The President was very friendly, very approachable, and very down to earth to my surprise. That was a very special moment for me. In all the times that I have been praying it was the first time I had been asked to pray for the President of the United States of America.

When the president was introduced by President Mark Morial, he said that Reverend Ernest Ferrell, President and CEO of the Tallahassee Urban League will offer prayer for the President of the United States. I was prepared to pray, but I must have taken a second or two too long to get started. The president standing behind me said, "Go on and start," and I did. I asked the Lord to bless President Bush with wisdom and knowledge and make him wise, help him to make wise decisions that will have a positive impact on our Nation and on the world. I prayed that the Lord would protect the president.

Our Nation needs a president who has close ties with a God who created us in His image and in His likeness.

Once I finished the prayer the president thanked me and addressed the conference. Those few moments with the Lord, on behalf of President George W. Bush, gave me a better appreciation for him and a closer walk with God because he recognized that to God it does not matter who you are or what level or position you hold. We all need God to bless us, because His love is available. When the dust settles we are all ashes to ashes and dust to dust, and where we will spend eternity is determined by our faith and our acceptance of the Lord in our life.

The challenges of leadership are embedded in my spiritual insight, wisdom, and knowledge that God has given me according to the ability I have to comprehend His word. I have been privileged to receive the abundance of His goodness and mercy, and surrendering all to Him, our Lord and Savior, Jesus Christ. To God be the glory for the things that He has done for us.

How Do the Pastor and CEO Complement Each Other?

I have been asked over and over for many years, how do you manage to pastor hundreds of members which requires an enormous amount of time, patience, and love while serving as president and CEO of the Tallahassee Urban League? The answer I give most of the time is simple, but I think profound. I have a unique opportunity to preach about what the Lord can do on any given day, particularly on Sunday. I preach that the Lord will make a way out of what we consider to be no way. I preach the Lord provides shelter from the storm; the Lord clothes the naked, gives sight to the blind, restores those who sit in the shadows of darkness unto the marvelous light; the Lord changed water to wine; and the Lord dramatically opened up the Red Sea and delivered the children of Israel across on dry land.

These are just a few of the things I preach about and have preached about over the last 50 years. What I found to be gratifying is that I can preach about what the Lord can do and then implement the teachings by providing through the Tallahassee Urban League. These things I preach about can be applied to individuals and families who need those services for food, shelter, counseling, clothes, and encouragement.

The Urban League has provided shelter from life storms to elderly families and individuals whose houses are substandard. Those elderly members of the family are on a fixed income and in some instances no income at all. For the most part all they really have is that little house that is substandard and does not meet the City's minimum requirement for a home not to be demolished. Those families do not have the resources to bring their homes up to standards and this is when the Urban League housing program provides help. Over 700 homes which fit that description have been rehabilitated by the Urban League since the program started years ago.

The Urban League housing program provides many other services related to housing to poor and disenfranchised individuals and families, such as first time home buyers workshops which assist individuals through educational workshops, and other direct services that assist in purchasing their first home. Once the workshop is completed they are eligible for down payment assistance. Over 5,000 individuals and families have graduated from this program. The housing counseling program for many years has implemented the Lord's promise that He would be a wonderful counselor. I hold these things true through our housing counseling program, because the Urban League is a certified housing counseling agency through HUD.

This program continues to implement the Lord's benefit programs which provide clients with foreclosure counseling, landlord tenant counseling, and other related counseling and housing needs. Over 20,000 clients in the Big Bend area were served or have been served over the years. We continue to implement the Lord's programs through our help to victims of crime and our victim witness service program that assists victims and families in coping with the trauma of a violent crime. Victims receive support and aid in filing the appropriate forms for compensation, referrals, personal advocacies, and crisis intervention of the things Jesus taught, and I preach about all of the things He promised in His word.

Mental health counseling is another issue that is so important in addressing the words of God through implementing these programs to assist those who have lost wages and disability assistance. In the event of death the advocate assists in filing for workman's comp, loss of support, and even funeral service arrangements. Implementing the Lord's work through these many services further includes our Black on Black crime prevention and intervention programs. The Black on Black crime convention program has been operating since 1985. The program's slogan is "Crime is not a part of our black heritage." Black on Black crime prevention has evolved into a major force in the services that the Urban League provides.

These services implement the Lord's work through educating the community on crime prevention and intervention, focusing on educating the community on how to protect themselves from those who are involved in criminal acts, and taking from those who are not able to protect themselves. The Urban League works together with law enforcement trying to bridge the gaps that so often are attributable to law enforcement.

The Urban League along with my responsibility in the church continues to work together to implement the services that the Lord provides us through the Urban League movement. The work continues with the Urban League Youth Crime Prevention Program as social responsibilities and character building programs. The Urban League is committed to the idea that preventing and intervening during the critical times in a youth's life will provide a stronger foundation for them to achieve a better quality of life.

The youth crime prevention and intervention and social responsibility program, as well as character building, provides assistance in the following areas: parenting skill training, tutoring, first time offenders programs, at risk youth programs, drop out prevention, Team Summit, and community bridge-building workshops. The social responsibility and character building provides a multi-faceted communication curriculum designed to assist and ease the transition of youth ages 10 through 16 from childhood to early adulthood.

The program conducts educational workshops which include conflict resolution, peer pressure education involving decision-making, anger management and aggression management, and much more. Everything this program does re-enforces spiritual values, touches the hearts and souls of the people I preach to and the services that are provided through the Urban League. I have served, over the years, in both areas with much success. They are tied together with complimentary value and substance, and that is what I tell those persons who ask, how do you do both of these jobs with enormous responsibilities. These two areas of my life alone are responsible for providing me with the enormous ability to enhance my spiritual challenges and my social responsibilities.

Through these unique programs, the opportunity and the experiences that have challenged me over the years, using my faith in God, and the hard work that is provided, I am deeply gratified for the results that both the church and CEO of the Urban League have had on so many individuals and families. To God I give the glory for providing me with the challenges and the experiences of leadership.

Urban League Song

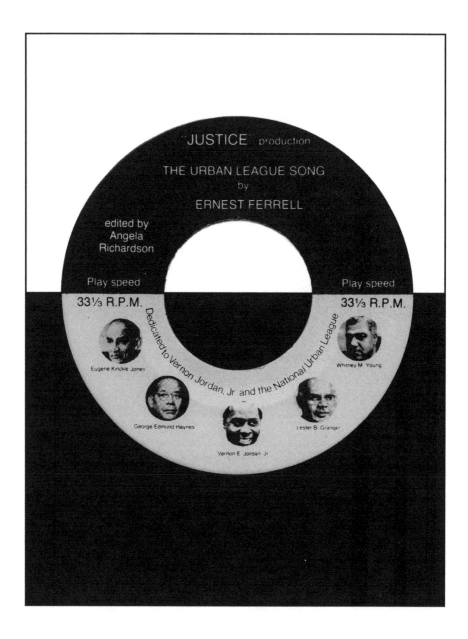

Words to the Urban League Song

Back in 1910, a new movement began when Southern Black Folks moved to northern land, for so long they knew nothing but hardship and strife, so they searched for freedom and a new way of life. They heard that the North promised better things like employment, sound housing and the peace that they bring, they heard of good health care for the whole family and about education of the best of quality. When they arrived and discovered things were not that good, not much better than the South, they would go home if they could. They cried out in anger as they thought of the past, Lord give us the strength to find justice at last. Their struggles were noticed, their cries were heard by concerned Black and White folks with their heart to observe. The movement they formed to ensure equality was The Urban League Movement, building for equality and opportunity. The Urban League continues to stand the rugged test of rebuilding our cities with equality at its best, so that Blacks would be able to fulfill their every dream and share America's riches, though remote they sometime seem, we must all live together, Black and White, rich and poor and in order to ensure this we must also share the fight. Our leaders paved the way for us and do so even now, Lester Granger, Whitney Young and Vernon Jordon, showed us how and with the help of local presidents, volunteers and staff have done. Our battle for equality and justice will be won.

LEADER	CHORUS
Justice will be won	Justice will be won
Justice will be won	Justice will be won
Justice will be won	Justice will be won
Justice will be won	Justice will be won

Conclusion

Preparing for and experiencing the challenges of leadership has been truly an experience that would not change in any way from the day I was born to the day I escaped death when my brother unknowingly sprayed me with a spray gun while I slept in my baby crib, and my mother saved my life when she discovered what my brother was actually doing.

I would not change the experiences that I went through at Waterville, New York, where we picked beans with our hands and caught fish on the banks of the river. The experiences that I went through during the summer vacation working in a restaurant in Miami, Florida, when an out of controll man threw a knife at another man and the knife landed in the back of my legs.

All of these events were a part of my development and who I am today. This book explains the challenges and experiences I went through and the developmental stages of my life that were all of God's plan for me to get where I am today and to have impacted the lives of so many people along the way.

It was no accident that my father and my mother had me and their DNA gave me life, and my spiritual development carried me through so many ups and downs, successes and failures. They were all necessary in order for me to prepare and meet many challenges that would develop over the years.

I was not sure when I was appointed to the Board of Directors of the Tallahassee Urban League, an organization that I had no idea as to what it was, what was its mission, and just how I would fit in. The Lord knew and He fitted me in and developed me into the leader of the Tallahassee Urban League for over 41 years.

Through the Urban League I developed the slogan, "We are making a difference" recognized throughout Tallahassee and surrounding communities. If I could receive a dollar from everyone who sang the slogan or of those who have asked me to sing it, I would be a rich man.

This Urban League movement has changed the lives for the better of thousands of individuals and families throughout the city, the county, and surrounding communities.

I am confident that my challenges and my experiences of leadership have made a positive difference in the lives of thousands in the church, and community, not only locally, but nationally as well. This book tells my story and my story is unique because of my dual role in the community as a pastor, and as an "Urban Leaguer." The many blessings that I have received have helped me to overcome many obstacles in life.

About the Author
Reverend Dr. Ernest Ferrell

A visionary faithful servant, community leader, treasured human resource, former president of the National Primitive Baptist Convention, USA, pastor of the St. Mary Primitive Baptist Church, president and CEO of the Tallahassee Urban League, well known in Leon County, Florida, and married to the former Mary E. Richardson. Attended the public schools of Leon County and graduated from Old Lincoln High School in 1962.

He was the first African American cashier to be employed by the Winn-Dixie Stores Company. He entered into the United States Army in 1966, and was honorably discharged in 1968. He earned a Bachelor of Science Degree in 1972, from Florida A&M University in Sociology and a minor in Corrections.

He excelled in three areas of leadership during his career, including church community, business community and the Urban League community. His leadership in the church began when he was a youth singing in the church choir. He sang in the Lincoln High School Glee Club and a gospel group called the Walls of Zion.

In 1972, he produced an album entitled "The Ferrells In Concert" with his brother and sister. From singing he progressed to the pulpit as a gospel preacher and was later ordained in 1969, to pastor the Galilee Primitive Baptist Church.

In 1992, he was called to pastor the St. Mary Primitive Baptist Church and installed as its pastor where he currently serves. He moved through in the ranks of the National Primitive Baptist Denomination where he served a successful three-year term as president of this 600,000 membership convention. In August 2008, he was re-elected to serve another three-year term as president of the convention.

In the business realm, his leadership includes proprietor of three small businesses in Tallahassee, Florida, Ferrell's Plaza, Hallie's Ice Cream & Sandwich Shop, and Ferrell's Restaurant.

Wife Mrs. Mary R. Ferrell and Rev Ernest Ferrell

He has successfully achieved the position of CEO of the Tallahassee Urban League. The Board of Directors appointed him to this position in 1973, where he has served with honor and distinction. Through his leadership at the Tallahassee Urban League, thousands of individuals and families in the Tallahassee and surrounding communities have received many services, including housing, crime prevention, youth services, victim rights assistance, emergency food and shelter and much more.

Reverend Ferrell received an honorary doctoral degree in Human Letters from his alma mater, Florida A&M University, and other numerous awards. The Omega Man of the Year Award, the Florida A&M University Martin Luther King Leadership Award, and the City of Tallahassee Business Leadership Award, to name a few.

Reverend Ernest Ferrell, a man of distinction who has earned many accolades over his life's journey and now he can add author to his repertoire. The author is a man of God, a man of high integrity, a man who recognized the needs of his community and worked to resolve them, and a man who put his trust in God and worked diligently everyday to make a difference in the lives of the people he serves.

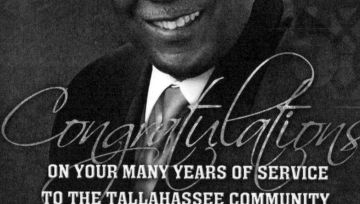

FLORIDA A&M UNIVERSITY

Congratulations

ON YOUR MANY YEARS OF SERVICE
TO THE TALLAHASSEE COMMUNITY.
AS AN ALUMNUS OF FAMU,
YOUR TIRELESS EFFORTS
TO IMPROVE THE LIVES OF OTHERS
IS GREATLY APPRECIATED.

ELDER DR. ERNEST FERRELL